THE PULPIT & THE PEOPLE

PATHWAY EDUCATIONAL RESOURCES

COMPLETE HECM RETIREMENT STRATEGY TOOLKIT

A Plain-Language Education and Planning System

FINANCE GUIDE | STRATEGY GUIDE | WORKBOOK

PREMIUM COLOR EDITION

Complete HECM
Retirement Strategy Toolkit

EDUCATION • PREPARATION • INFORMED ACTION

Complete HECM Retirement Strategy Toolkit

A comprehensive guide to home equity, retirement strategy, household preparation, and responsible implementation

Prepared by
Tyrone Simpson
Pathway Educational Resources

ISBN 979-8-9967481-2-9

PUBLICATION INFORMATION

Copyright & Edition Record

COPYRIGHT

PUBLISHER

The Pulpit & The People, through Pathway Educational Resources.

ISBN

979-8-9967481-2-9 - Complete HECM Retirement Strategy Toolkit, premium-color paperback edition.

PERMISSIONS

TRADEMARKS

EDITION

First edition, September 2026. Program rules, limits, costs, and guidance may change after publication.

READ BEFORE USE

Master Educational Notice

This toolkit helps readers organize questions and prepare for conversations. It does not replace individualized professional advice.

EDUCATIONAL USE ONLY

This publication is not a loan application, lender quote, financial plan, investment recommendation, legal opinion, tax advice, insurance recommendation, or guarantee of HECM eligibility or proceeds.

VERIFY CURRENT PROGRAM INFORMATION

HECM eligibility, principal limits, rates, costs, property standards, counseling, financial assessment, and borrower obligations must be confirmed through current written information from qualified professionals.

ONGOING HOMEOWNER OBLIGATIONS

Borrowers generally retain title but must continue meeting loan requirements, including principal-residence occupancy, property taxes, homeowners insurance, applicable assessments, and home maintenance.

EXAMPLES ARE ILLUSTRATIVE

Households, organizations, property values, dollar amounts, timelines, projections, and insurance concepts in the strategy section are fictional or generalized. Replace every assumption with verified facts.

INDEPENDENT REVIEW MATTERS

Consult an independent HUD-approved housing counselor, an FHA-approved lender, and appropriate legal, tax, estate, insurance, and financial professionals before acting.

ORIENTATION

How to Use This Toolkit

Work through the three parts in sequence, but return to the worksheets whenever household facts change.

1. **Learn the framework**

   Begin with Part I to understand what a HECM is, what it is not, and which questions establish readiness.

2. **Study the decision process**

   Use Part II to see how goals, cash flow, home equity, insurance, estate planning, and implementation responsibilities fit together.

3. **Complete the workbook**

   Record your household information in Part III. Use current statements and write down the source and date for important figures.

4. **Bring the book to meetings**

   Use your completed pages during counseling and professional consultations. Record answers, documents requested, and follow-up dates.

5. **Compare alternatives**

   Do not evaluate a HECM in isolation. Compare it with downsizing, refinancing, budget changes, assistance programs, and other appropriate strategies.

6. **Review annually**

   Update income, expenses, insurance, property charges, home condition, family goals, and professional contacts at least once each year.

NAVIGATION

Contents

NAVIGATION

Contents - Continued

MASTER INTRODUCTION

A Responsible Retirement-Finance Process

Home equity can be a powerful resource. The quality of the outcome depends on the quality of the questions, verification, and long-term preparation surrounding it.

A HECM should never be reduced to a single question such as, "How much can I receive?" A stronger process begins with the household's goals, monthly budget, expected years in the home, property obligations, health and caregiving needs, spouse protections, and legacy priorities.

This toolkit brings education, strategy, and practical preparation into one system. Part I establishes plain-language foundations. Part II demonstrates how an appealing idea must be tested, redesigned, documented, and coordinated. Part III gives the household room to organize the facts that professionals will need.

The central principle is sustainability: use the smallest responsible amount and structure that accomplishes a clearly stated objective while preserving flexibility for the future. Every important assumption should be replaced with written, current, professional information before a decision is made.

THE PATHWAY STANDARD

Understand the program. Organize the household. Compare alternatives. Verify every number. Coordinate the professionals. Document the decision. Review the plan every year.

THE PROBLEMS WE ADDRESS

What This Book Helps You Solve

A HECM is not a universal solution. This compendium helps eligible homeowners understand and test several practical retirement-finance opportunities.

1. **Look beyond a single credit score**

   Credit score alone is not the determining factor. The lender completes a broader financial assessment, including property-charge history, income, assets, obligations, and willingness and capacity to meet ongoing responsibilities.

2. **Address immediate cash needs**

   Explore whether verified HECM proceeds could help pay an existing mortgage, establish reserves, fund necessary repairs, or meet other documented needs.

3. **Remove required monthly mortgage payments**

   A HECM generally eliminates required monthly principal-and-interest payments, while taxes, insurance, assessments, occupancy, and maintenance obligations remain.

4. **Choose how funds are received**

   Compare available structures such as a lump sum, line of credit, scheduled advances, or combinations, subject to current program rules and loan terms.

5. **Create an heir-retention strategy**

   Prepare heirs to evaluate payoff, refinance, sale, insurance, reserves, or other lawful options if keeping the home is a family goal.

6. **Build retirement resilience**

   Use home equity carefully alongside savings, income, expense reductions, reserves, and professional advice rather than treating borrowing as the entire nest egg.

7. **Follow a simple planning system**

   Organize income, expenses, property charges, documents, scenarios, professional questions, and annual reviews in one practical workbook.

PART I

HECM Retirement Finance Foundations

A plain-language introduction to readiness, program basics, borrower responsibilities, costs, counseling, and next-step questions.

PATHWAY
INVESTMENTS 101, LLC

About This Guide

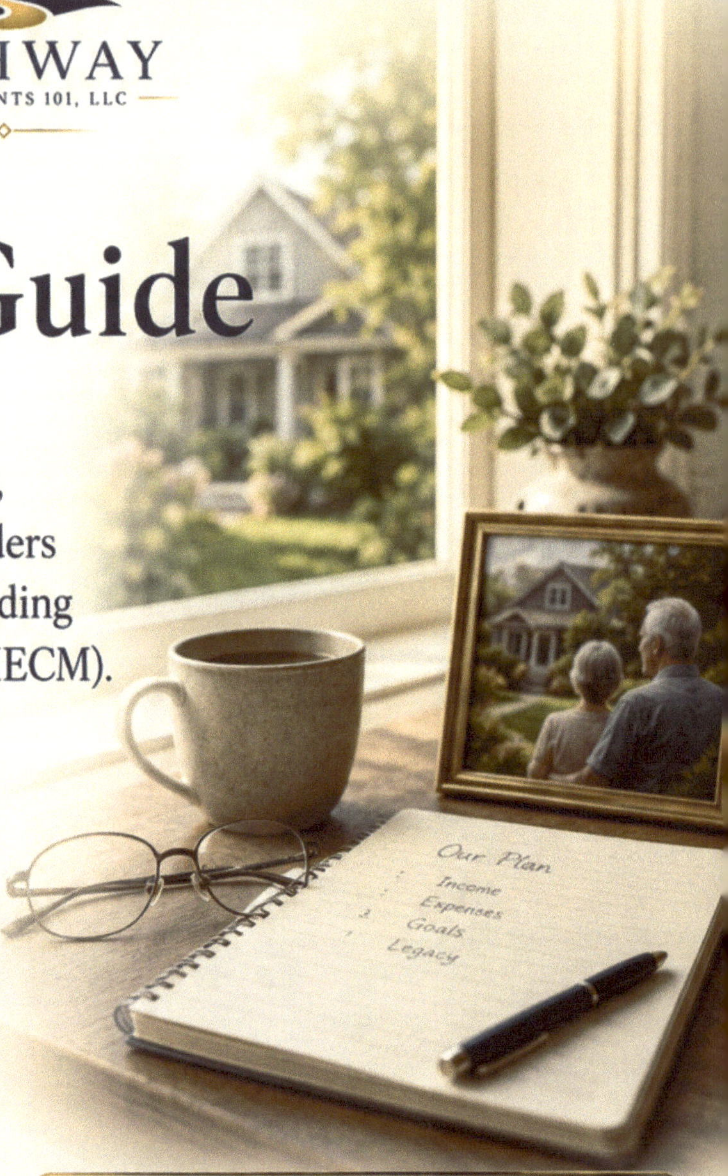

This guide helps homeowners, spouses, adult children, pastors, and church leaders understand the planning issues surrounding a Home Equity Conversion Mortgage (HECM).

How to Use This Book

1. Read the overview pages first.
2. Gather income, expense, and property information.
3. Review the risks, obligations, and legacy issues.
4. Use the companion workbook to test real numbers.
5. Discuss the results with qualified professionals.

Important Notice

This guide is an educational resource only. It is not legal, tax, mortgage, insurance, or investment advice.

PATHWAY
INVESTMENTS 101, LLC

Reverse Mortgage Readiness Checklist

Use this checklist before you begin comparing lenders or making a final decision.

1. ☐ Confirm that the homeowner is age 62 or older.
2. ☐ Confirm that the property will be the principal residence.
3. ☐ Review title status and any existing liens.
4. ☐ Estimate property taxes, homeowners insurance, and maintenance costs.
5. ☐ Organize monthly income and expense information.
6. ☐ Discuss goals with a spouse, heirs, or trusted family members.
7. ☐ Schedule HUD-approved reverse mortgage counseling.
8. ☐ Compare written lender quotes and payout options.

PATHWAY

INVESTMENTS 101, LLC

Reverse Mortgage 101

What It Is — and What It Is Not

What It Is

- An FHA-insured reverse mortgage for eligible older homeowners.
- A way to convert part of home equity into usable funds.
- A product that may offer a lump sum, line of credit, monthly payments, or a combination.
- A loan with no required monthly principal-and-interest payment while obligations are met.

What It Is Not

- It is not free money.
- It is not a substitute for tax, estate, or legal planning.
- It does not eliminate taxes, insurance, or home-maintenance duties.
- It is not automatically the best option for every family or every legacy goal.

Key idea: *the right question is not 'Can I get one?' but 'Does it fit my long-term plan?'*

PATHWAY
INVESTMENTS 101, LLC

Household Cash Flow & Living Standards

Cash-flow planning helps families see the full picture of their financial reality. It reveals whether a reverse mortgage could relieve pressure, maintain stability, or create new strain over time. By comparing income and expenses, you can make confident decisions that protect your home and your way of life.

Core Planning Categories

Income
Social Security, pensions, work income, annuities, and other recurring funds.

Fixed Expenses
Housing costs, insurance, taxes, debt payments, and utilities.

Variable Expenses
Food, transportation, healthcare, personal care, and family support.

Monthly Gap or Surplus
The difference between income and expenses.

Questions to Ask

- What happens if income drops by 10% or 20%?
- What happens if healthcare or property costs rise?
- How much cushion remains each month?
- Which expenses are essential and which are optional?

PATHWAY
INVESTMENTS 101, LLC

Borrower Responsibilities & Key Risks

1 Ongoing Responsibilities

- Live in the home as the principal residence.
- Pay property taxes on time.
- Maintain homeowners insurance and any required hazard coverage.
- Keep the property in reasonable repair.
- Respond promptly to lender requests for required occupancy certifications.

2 Key Risks to Understand

- Loan balances can grow over time because interest and fees accrue.
- Home equity may decline more quickly than expected.
- A surviving spouse or heirs may face difficult decisions if the plan is not documented well.
- Inadequate cash reserves can create stress even when no monthly mortgage payment is required.

A reverse mortgage can reduce payment pressure, but it does not remove the need for financial discipline.

Insurance Coordination & Legacy Planning

Some families explore life insurance as one possible tool to support legacy goals. However, affordability, insurability, policy design, and long-term fit must be reviewed carefully before moving forward.

Key Evaluation Questions

- Is the policy affordable over time?
- Is the death benefit likely to support the intended legacy goal?
- Is the policy guaranteed or could it lapse?
- Who should own the policy and who should be the beneficiary?
- How does the policy coordinate with the broader estate plan?

Important Reminder

- Insurance should not be treated as an automatic fix.
- The growing loan balance should be compared against the intended benefit.
- Families should involve qualified insurance, legal, and tax professionals.

Sample Scenario Snapshot

This illustration uses sample data to show how a household might compare debt growth, home value, and legacy goals over time.

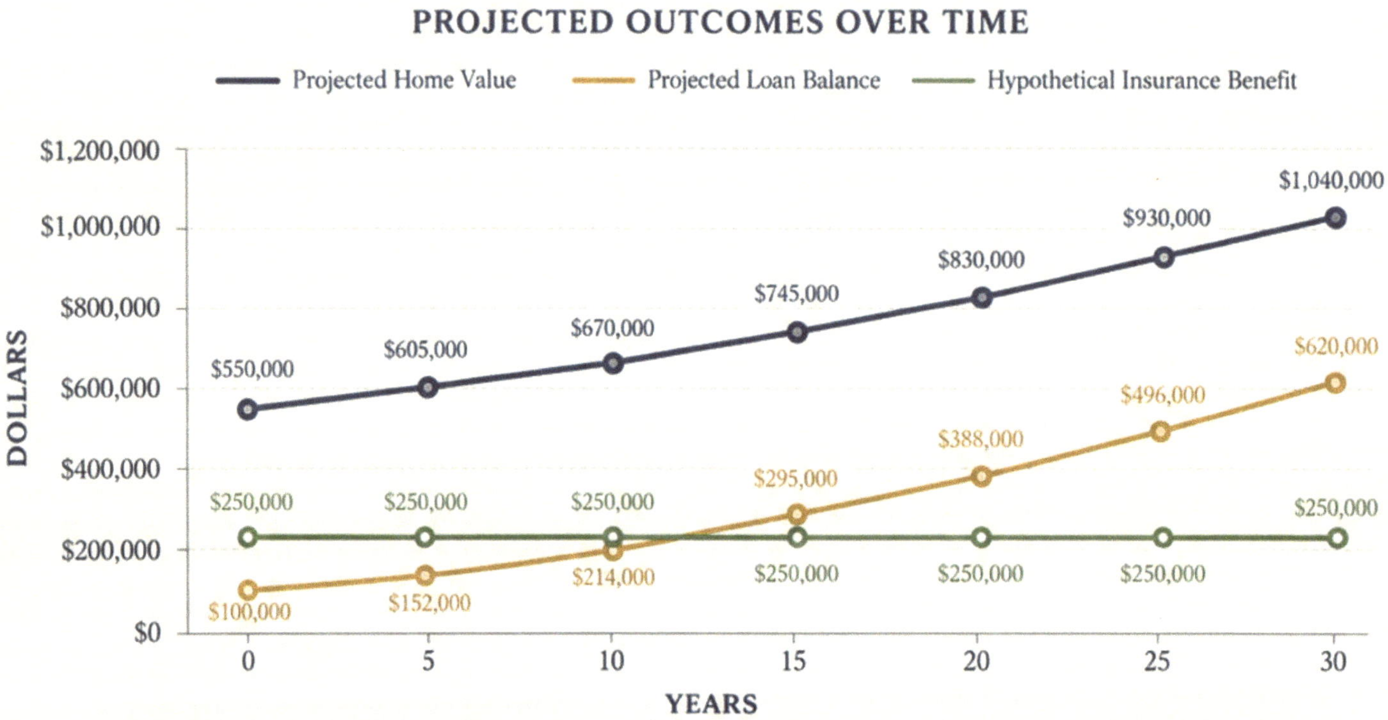

THREE TAKEAWAYS

- Lower available income can lead to larger reverse-mortgage draws.
- Larger draws can accelerate future loan-balance growth.
- Legacy planning works best when affordability and long-term projections are reviewed together.

Illustrative example only — not a lender quote or guarantee.

PATHWAY
INVESTMENTS 101, LLC

Stress-Test Your Plan

Stress testing helps families see how the plan may respond if income decreases, expenses rise, or cash reserves become tighter. This process identifies vulnerabilities early so adjustments can be made with confidence.

How Different Scenarios Affect Your Plan Over Time

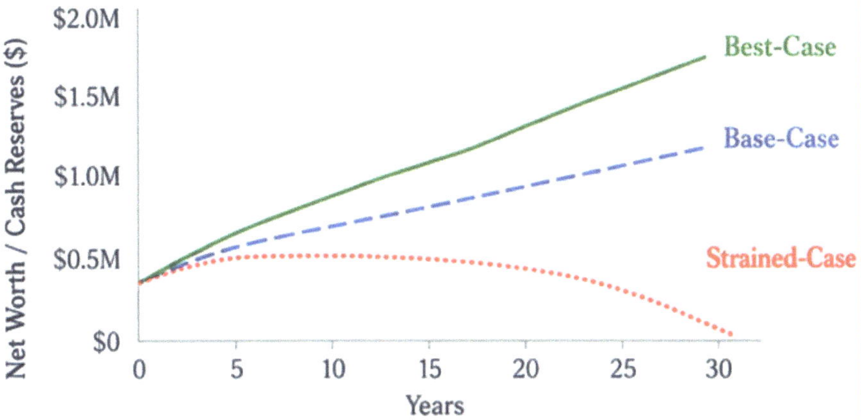

Scenario	Key Assumptions	30-Year Outcome
Best-Case	Income grows, expenses stay controlled	$1.7M
Base-Case	Moderate growth, typical inflation	$1.1M
Strained-Case	Income drops, expenses rise, cash reserves tighten	$0

Practical Stress Tests

1. Reduce household income by 10%.
2. Reduce household income by 20%.
3. Increase property and healthcare expenses.
4. Compare best-case, base-case, and strained-case outcomes.

Goal: find the point where lifestyle, property obligations, or legacy goals become strained.

PATHWAY
INVESTMENTS 101, LLC

7-Step Implementation Path

A thoughtful implementation process helps families move from curiosity to clarity.

1. **Clarify goals.**
Define your retirement goals, legacy intentions, and financial priorities.

2. **Gather household and property data.**
Collect income, expenses, debts, and property information.

3. **Run the planning workbook.**
Complete the workbook and review your cash-flow picture.

4. **Complete HUD-approved counseling.**
Meet with a HUD-approved reverse mortgage counselor for guidance.

5. **Compare lender quotes and payout options.**
Evaluate terms, costs, and payout structures to find the best fit.

6. **Review insurance and estate-planning coordination.**
Confirm insurance needs and coordinate with your estate plan.

7. **Make a documented final decision.**
Choose the option that aligns with your goals and document your decision.

Companion Workbook Overview & Next Steps

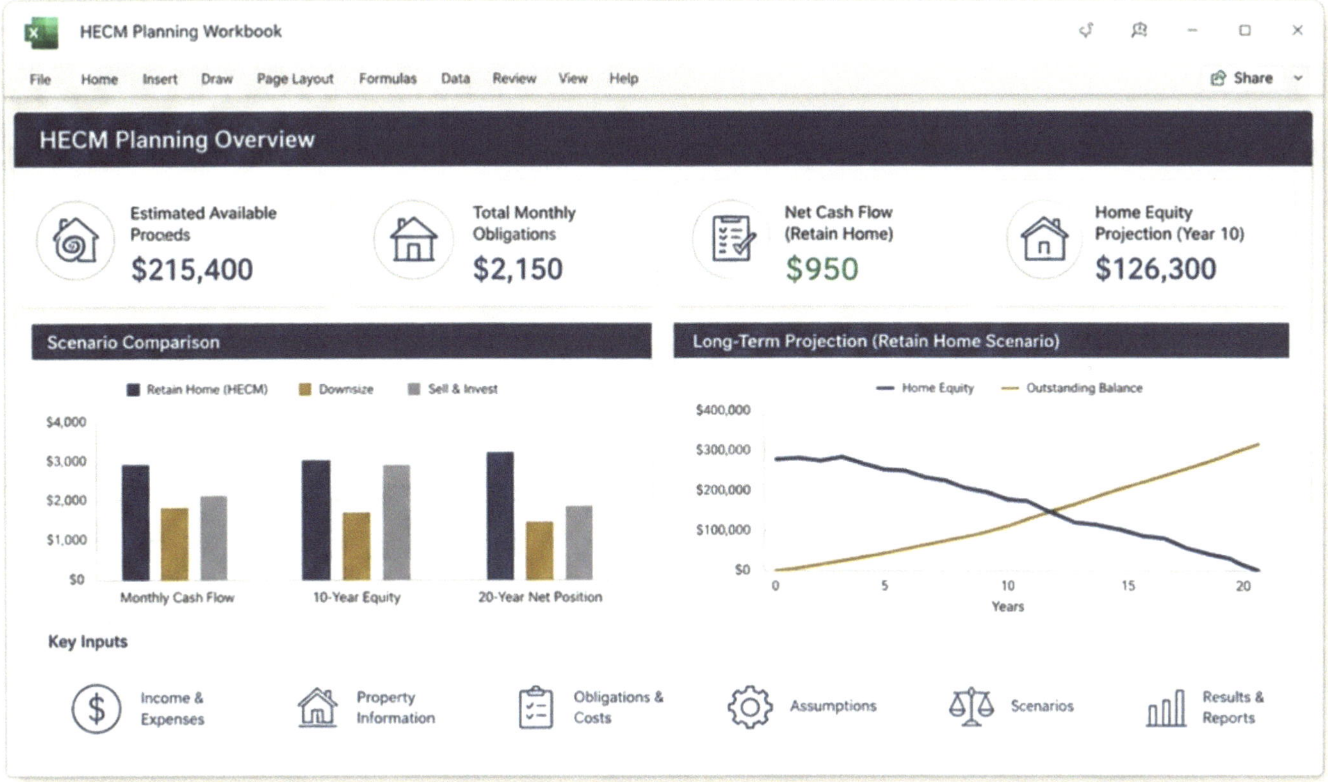

What the Workbook Helps You Do

- Organize income, expenses, and property obligations.
- Compare scenarios and estimate budget pressure.
- Review long-term projections and planning assumptions.
- Prepare more informed conversations with professionals.

Next Steps

- Enter verified numbers into the workbook.
- Update key assumptions carefully.
- Review results with a spouse or family members.
- Consult qualified mortgage, insurance, legal, and tax professionals.

The workbook turns this guide from theory into real-number planning.

PART I - EXPANDED DECISION GUIDE

HECM Mechanics: The Loan Beneath the Headlines

Understand the legal and financial structure before evaluating benefits.

What stays the same

A HECM is a mortgage secured by the home. The homeowner keeps title; the lender does not become the owner simply because a reverse mortgage is recorded.

- The home remains the borrower's principal residence while the loan is active.
- Property taxes, homeowners insurance, applicable flood insurance, association charges, and maintenance remain household responsibilities.
- The borrower can generally sell the home at any time; the HECM balance is then repaid from sale proceeds or other funds.

What changes

Unlike a traditional amortizing mortgage, scheduled monthly principal-and-interest payments are generally not required. Interest, mortgage-insurance charges, and financed costs are added to the balance instead.

- The amount owed can rise over time even when the borrower satisfies all homeowner obligations.
- Home equity may decline as the loan balance rises, depending on home appreciation, draws, interest, and time.
- The loan typically becomes due after the last borrower or eligible non-borrowing spouse dies, sells, or no longer occupies the home as required.

KEY IDEA
A HECM changes the timing of repayment; it does not eliminate repayment. The planning question is whether using home equity now improves the household's long-term stability enough to justify the cost and reduction in future equity.

Official source note: HUD HECM program materials; HUD housing-counseling guidance; and CFPB reverse-mortgage consumer guidance. Verify current rules and limits.

LOAN BALANCE

How the Loan Balance Changes Over Time

The balance grows as advances, interest, mortgage insurance, and financed costs accumulate.

Start with the opening balance

At closing, the HECM may pay off an existing mortgage and may finance eligible closing costs. Any cash or line-of-credit advance also becomes part of the balance.

Then add ongoing charges

Each month, interest is charged on the outstanding balance. FHA mortgage-insurance charges and any applicable servicing amounts may also be added according to the loan terms.

Draws accelerate balance growth

A borrower who takes $10,000 today begins accruing loan costs on that advance. A borrower who leaves funds undrawn generally does not pay interest on money that has not been borrowed.

Equity is the moving difference

Future equity depends on both sides of the equation: home value and loan balance. A growing home value can offset some balance growth, but appreciation is never guaranteed.

PLANNING STANDARD

Request a written year-by-year loan-balance illustration from the lender. Compare it with at least one lower-draw scenario and one non-HECM alternative. Do not rely on a verbal estimate.

Official source note: HUD HECM program materials; HUD housing-counseling guidance; and CFPB reverse-mortgage consumer guidance. Verify current rules and limits.

PROCEEDS

What Determines Available HECM Proceeds

Home value is only one input; age, rates, obligations, and program limits matter.

HUD explains that the amount available for withdrawal depends on the age of the youngest borrower or eligible non-borrowing spouse, current interest rates, and the lesser of the appraised value, the applicable HECM FHA mortgage limit, or - for a purchase - the sales price. Existing liens and financed charges reduce the net amount available.

Factor	Why it matters	Planning question
Youngest applicable age	Age is part of the principal-limit calculation.	Whose age controls the calculation?
Expected/current rate inputs	Higher rate assumptions can reduce available proceeds.	What rate is used for the principal-limit calculation?
Home value / FHA limit	Program calculations use the lesser applicable amount.	What value and program limit are being used?
Existing mortgage or liens	Mandatory payoff uses part of available proceeds.	How much remains after all required payoffs?
Closing costs / set-asides	Financed charges reduce net proceeds available to the household.	What is gross vs. net available cash?

2026 REFERENCE POINT
For FHA case numbers assigned in calendar year 2026, HUD lists a nationwide HECM maximum claim amount of $1,249,125. This is not an automatic loan amount. Verify the current-year limit before publication updates or borrower decisions.

Official source note: HUD HECM program materials; HUD housing-counseling guidance; and CFPB reverse-mortgage consumer guidance. Verify current rules and limits.

ELIGIBILITY

Borrower Eligibility: More Than Age 62

Age opens the door; the complete file must still satisfy program and underwriting requirements.

Core borrower conditions

- At least one borrower must meet the HECM age requirement; current HUD/CFPB consumer guidance describes HECMs as available to homeowners age 62 and older.
- The property must be the principal residence.
- An existing mortgage must generally be paid off at or before HECM closing using HECM proceeds or other funds.
- Federal debts and delinquent obligations can affect the transaction and may need resolution under current program rules.

Readiness conditions

- HUD-approved HECM counseling is required before the loan can proceed.
- The lender performs a financial assessment to evaluate whether the borrower can sustain property charges and other obligations.
- The property must meet applicable FHA standards, or required repairs must be addressed under permitted procedures.
- All owners, spouses, trusts, liens, and occupancy facts should be disclosed early; title surprises can derail the process.

DO NOT SELF-QUALIFY

A checklist can identify questions, but it cannot determine approval. Eligibility is confirmed through current HUD rules, counseling, property review, and lender underwriting.

Official source note: HUD HECM program materials; HUD housing-counseling guidance; and CFPB reverse-mortgage consumer guidance. Verify current rules and limits.

PROPERTY REVIEW

Property Eligibility & Condition

A retirement strategy cannot be stronger than the property facts beneath it.

Confirm the property type

Eligible property types depend on current FHA rules. Single-family homes and certain owner-occupied multi-unit properties may qualify; condominium and manufactured-home eligibility can require additional program-specific review.

Confirm principal residence

A HECM is designed around the borrower's principal residence. Extended absences, occupancy changes, or a permanent move can affect the loan. Keep records and ask the servicer how occupancy certification works.

Surface repair issues early

Appraisal or property review may identify conditions that must be corrected. Delaying known roof, electrical, plumbing, structural, safety, or insurance issues can create closing surprises.

Map recurring property charges

Taxes, homeowners insurance, flood insurance when applicable, association fees, special assessments, and maintenance belong in the retirement budget before the loan is selected.

PROPERTY TEST

Ask: If we remove the current mortgage payment but continue every property charge and realistic maintenance reserve, is this home still affordable for the next five to ten years?

Official source note: HUD HECM program materials; HUD housing-counseling guidance; and CFPB reverse-mortgage consumer guidance. Verify current rules and limits.

COUNSELING

HUD-Approved Counseling: What It Is Designed to Do

Counseling is an independent education step - not a lender sales appointment.

What the session should help clarify

- How HECMs work, including costs, repayment, property obligations, and alternatives.
- How the contemplated loan may affect the borrower's finances and housing plan.
- Questions involving spouses, heirs, occupancy, and long-term sustainability.
- Whether other public benefits, housing options, or financial strategies deserve consideration.

How to prepare

- Bring a current mortgage statement, property-tax information, insurance costs, income, recurring expenses, and household goals.
- Write down the amount of cash you actually need and why.
- Ask the counselor to explain any term you cannot repeat back in plain language.
- Treat the counseling certificate as completion of education - not as a guarantee of loan approval or suitability.

MEETING DISCIPLINE

Do not let the counseling appointment become a box to check. Use it to challenge assumptions before money, title, or family expectations become difficult to unwind.

Official source note: HUD HECM program materials; HUD housing-counseling guidance; and CFPB reverse-mortgage consumer guidance. Verify current rules and limits.

FINANCIAL ASSESSMENT

The Ability to Sustain the Home

The lender looks beyond equity to the borrower's capacity and willingness to meet ongoing obligations.

Why the assessment exists

A HECM removes the requirement for scheduled monthly principal-and-interest payments, but it does not remove property taxes, insurance, maintenance, or other household expenses. HUD requires a financial assessment so the lender can evaluate whether those obligations are likely to remain sustainable.

What the lender may review

Income, assets, credit history, property-charge payment history, recurring debt, and other documented obligations may be part of the analysis. Current lender and HUD requirements control the final documentation.

Residual income matters

The central planning issue is not simply whether the home contains enough equity. It is whether the household retains enough dependable cash flow after essential expenses to protect the property and live safely.

Weak cash flow is a warning, not a reason to borrow more

If the plan only works by assuming larger and larger future draws, the HECM may be postponing a structural budget problem rather than solving it.

HOUSEHOLD TEST

Complete the workbook with conservative income and expense assumptions before reviewing lender proceeds. The retirement budget should drive the borrowing decision - not the maximum amount available.

Official source note: HUD HECM program materials; HUD housing-counseling guidance; and CFPB reverse-mortgage consumer guidance. Verify current rules and limits.

PROPERTY-CHARGE SET-ASIDE

LESA: When Property Charges Are Set Aside

A Life Expectancy Set-Aside can change both cash availability and how taxes or insurance are funded.

What a LESA does

A Life Expectancy Set-Aside (LESA) reserves a portion of HECM proceeds for certain property charges, generally taxes and insurance, based on the lender's financial assessment and current HUD rules.

- A fully funded or partially funded set-aside may be required depending on the assessment.
- Funds committed to the set-aside are not the same as freely available cash proceeds.
- The set-aside can reduce the net amount available for other retirement goals.

Questions to ask

- Is a LESA required in this case? Why?
- Which property charges will it cover and which remain the borrower's direct responsibility?
- How much of the principal limit is reserved?
- How does the set-aside affect the line of credit, monthly payments, or other proceeds?
- What happens if taxes or insurance increase more than assumed?

PLAIN-LANGUAGE RULE

Do not describe a LESA as free money or an extra benefit. It is a structured use of loan proceeds intended to support payment of specified property charges.

Official source note: HUD HECM program materials; HUD housing-counseling guidance; and CFPB reverse-mortgage consumer guidance. Verify current rules and limits.

ONGOING OBLIGATIONS

Property Charges, Occupancy & Maintenance

A HECM can remain in place only while the household continues meeting the loan conditions.

Property taxes and insurance

Keep taxes and homeowners insurance current. Flood insurance may also be required when applicable. Failure to maintain required property charges can lead to default and potentially foreclosure.

Principal residence

The borrower generally must occupy the property as the principal residence. Health-care absences and other extended absences can have special rules; contact the servicer promptly rather than guessing.

Reasonable maintenance

The home must be maintained in a condition consistent with loan and property requirements. A realistic repair reserve belongs in the retirement plan.

Communication with the servicer

Open mail, respond to occupancy certifications, keep contact information current, and document conversations. Many preventable problems begin when notices are ignored.

ANNUAL REVIEW

Once a year, update taxes, insurance premiums, association charges, repair needs, emergency cash, HECM balance, available credit, and family contact information.

Official source note: HUD HECM program materials; HUD housing-counseling guidance; and CFPB reverse-mortgage consumer guidance. Verify current rules and limits.

COSTS

Understanding HECM Costs

Separate one-time closing costs from the costs that accumulate over time.

CFPB notes that reverse mortgages can be more expensive than other home loans. Costs vary by lender and transaction. The purpose of this page is to identify the categories that should appear in written estimates - not to predict a specific borrower's charges.

Cost category	When it appears	Why it matters
Origination fee	Closing	Compensation to the lender, subject to applicable limits.
Appraisal / title / recording / third-party charges	Closing	Transaction and property-review costs.
Initial FHA mortgage-insurance premium	Closing	Finances FHA insurance protection when permitted.
Interest	Over time	Accrues on the outstanding loan balance.
Annual mortgage-insurance charge	Over time	Added based on current program terms and outstanding balance.
Servicing-related amounts, if applicable	Over time	Review the actual lender disclosure and servicing structure.

Financing costs is still borrowing

When closing costs are financed, the borrower avoids paying them in cash at closing - but those costs become part of the loan balance and can accrue interest over time.

COST DISCIPLINE

Do not compare lenders only by the cash they say you can receive. Compare total costs, rate structure, draw plan, projected balance, and the amount of equity likely to remain under several scenarios.

Official source note: HUD HECM program materials; HUD housing-counseling guidance; and CFPB reverse-mortgage consumer guidance. Verify current rules and limits.

INTEREST-RATE STRUCTURE

Fixed, Adjustable & Expected Rate

The rate structure affects proceeds, payment-plan flexibility, and future loan-balance growth.

Fixed-rate structure

A fixed-rate HECM is commonly associated with a lump-sum distribution. The precise options and first-year limits depend on current program rules and the lender's product.

- Rate certainty does not mean balance certainty; draws, financed costs, and mortgage-insurance charges still affect the amount owed.
- Taking more money earlier generally causes more interest to accrue over time.

Adjustable-rate structure

Adjustable HECMs can support payment plans such as a line of credit, monthly tenure or term payments, or combinations, subject to program and lender terms.

- The note rate can change according to the index and margin stated in the loan documents.
- The expected rate used in principal-limit calculations is not necessarily the same thing as the current note rate.
- Ask for both current-rate and stress-rate balance illustrations.

RATE QUESTION

Do not ask only, "What is today's rate?" Ask which rate affects available proceeds, which rate accrues on the balance, how often it can adjust, what caps apply, and how the payment plan can change.

Official source note: HUD HECM program materials; HUD housing-counseling guidance; and CFPB reverse-mortgage consumer guidance. Verify current rules and limits.

DRAW STRATEGY

Accessing Proceeds: Choose the Use Before the Product

Match the withdrawal method to the household need instead of defaulting to the maximum cash available.

HECM proceeds can be structured in different ways depending on the loan type and current program rules. A good draw strategy uses the least borrowing necessary to accomplish a defined retirement objective.

Need	Possible approach to evaluate	Primary risk to test
One-time mandatory payoff	Closing draw / required payoff	Large opening balance reduces future equity.
Emergency liquidity	Line of credit	Access rules, variable rates, and long-term costs.
Recurring cash-flow gap	Term or tenure payments	Budget may still fail if property charges or living costs rise.
Defined home repair	Targeted draw	Project overruns and contractor pressure.
Mixed needs	Combination plan	Complexity; understand which dollars are borrowed and when.

STRATEGY RULE

Borrowing capacity is not a spending target. Write the purpose of every planned draw in the workbook and identify what would cause you to stop or reduce future borrowing.

Official source note: HUD HECM program materials; HUD housing-counseling guidance; and CFPB reverse-mortgage consumer guidance. Verify current rules and limits.

LINE OF CREDIT

The HECM Line of Credit

Flexible access can be valuable, but the growth feature is not investment income or a bank deposit.

Use only what is needed

With an adjustable-rate HECM line of credit, interest generally accrues on amounts actually borrowed rather than on the unused available credit.

Understand the growth feature

CFPB materials explain that unused credit can grow over time under the HECM formula. This growth increases future borrowing capacity; it is not interest paid to the homeowner and it is not cash sitting in a savings account.

Protect the purpose

A standby line can support emergency planning, but easy access can also encourage spending that was never part of the retirement plan.

Track available credit and balance separately

The amount available to draw and the amount already owed are different figures. Request current statements and review both.

LANGUAGE MATTERS

Avoid saying the line of credit "earns interest." A more accurate description is that unused borrowing capacity may grow under the HECM formula, subject to the loan terms and continued availability of the program.

Official source note: HUD HECM program materials; HUD housing-counseling guidance; and CFPB reverse-mortgage consumer guidance. Verify current rules and limits.

MONTHLY PAYMENT PLANS

Tenure and Term: Income Support Without Calling It Income

Monthly HECM advances are loan proceeds, not earnings, wages, or a pension.

Tenure plan

A tenure payment plan can provide monthly advances while the borrower remains eligible and the HECM remains in force, according to the loan terms.

- Useful to evaluate when the household has a persistent monthly cash-flow gap.
- The payment should not distract from rising property charges or other long-term expenses.
- Ask how changing the payment plan affects available credit and future advances.

Term plan

A term plan provides monthly advances for a defined period selected under the loan structure.

- Useful to evaluate for a temporary bridge, such as a planned five-year period.
- A temporary payment does not solve a permanent structural deficit unless another resource replaces it later.
- Build a "what happens after the term ends?" line into the retirement plan.

TAX LANGUAGE

HECM advances are borrowed funds, not earned income. Tax treatment can depend on the transaction and household circumstances; consult a qualified tax professional rather than relying on general statements.

Official source note: HUD HECM program materials; HUD housing-counseling guidance; and CFPB reverse-mortgage consumer guidance. Verify current rules and limits.

LUMP SUM

Lump Sum & Initial-Disbursement Discipline

Large immediate access can solve a defined problem - or create avoidable long-term cost.

Use a written purpose

A lump sum should have a specific job: required mortgage payoff, defined repair, debt restructuring, or another documented purpose that has been independently evaluated.

Understand first-year limits

HECM rules can restrict the amount available during the initial disbursement period. Mandatory obligations can affect the calculation. Request the lender's written explanation for the exact case.

Avoid “cash because it is available”

Borrowed cash placed in a low-yield account may create a negative spread while interest and insurance charges accumulate on the HECM balance.

Protect against pressure

Be cautious when a contractor, salesperson, investment promoter, family member, or other third party pushes a reverse mortgage primarily to fund their product or transaction.

LUMP-SUM TEST

Would the household still choose this expenditure if the cost were described as “home equity borrowed today plus years of interest and fees”? If not, reconsider the draw.

Official source note: HUD HECM program materials; HUD housing-counseling guidance; and CFPB reverse-mortgage consumer guidance. Verify current rules and limits.

EXISTING MORTGAGE

Using a HECM to Pay Off a Current Mortgage

Eliminating a monthly mortgage payment can improve cash flow, but it uses home equity and replaces one debt structure with another.

Potential benefit

- Removes the required monthly principal-and-interest payment on the existing mortgage after it is paid off, assuming the HECM remains in good standing.
- Can improve monthly cash flow for a household whose mortgage payment is the dominant retirement expense.
- May reduce the risk of missing a traditional mortgage payment during a future income shock.

Tradeoffs to measure

- The existing payoff consumes part of the HECM principal limit and increases the opening HECM balance.
- Property taxes, insurance, maintenance, and other charges remain.
- If the current mortgage balance is high relative to HECM proceeds, the borrower may need cash at closing or may not have meaningful remaining proceeds.
- Compare with refinancing, downsizing, sale-and-rent, or other housing strategies.

CASH-FLOW MATH

Calculate the exact monthly payment eliminated, then compare it with the estimated reduction in future equity and the household's expected years in the home. The answer is about retirement utility, not simply debt removal.

Official source note: HUD HECM program materials; HUD housing-counseling guidance; and CFPB reverse-mortgage consumer guidance. Verify current rules and limits.

HECM FOR PURCHASE

A Different Retirement Path: HECM for Purchase

Some older buyers use a HECM to purchase a new principal residence rather than remain in the current home.

How the concept works

CFPB describes HECM for Purchase as a program that allows eligible borrowers age 62 or older to combine HECM proceeds with cash or equity from another source to buy a new principal residence.

Why families consider it

A household may prefer a smaller, safer, lower-maintenance, single-story, or more accessible home. Using HECM for Purchase can be evaluated as an alternative to buying entirely with cash or taking a traditional mortgage.

Cash is still required

The buyer must bring enough funds to cover the difference between the HECM proceeds and the purchase price, plus applicable closing costs. Not every property qualifies.

Do not compare homes only by purchase price

Compare taxes, insurance, association fees, maintenance, accessibility, distance to family and health care, and expected years of occupancy.

STRATEGIC QUESTION

Could moving to a more suitable home improve retirement stability more than borrowing against the current home? Include HECM for Purchase in the alternatives discussion when relocation is already on the table.

Official source note: HUD HECM program materials; HUD housing-counseling guidance; and CFPB reverse-mortgage consumer guidance. Verify current rules and limits.

SPOUSE PROTECTION

Spouses & Non-Borrowing Spouses

The names on the loan, ages, occupancy history, and marriage status can have major consequences later.

Co-borrower protection

When spouses are co-borrowers, both are borrowers under the HECM and both must comply with the loan obligations.

- The age of the youngest borrower can affect proceeds.
- A surviving co-borrower can generally continue the HECM if the loan remains in good standing and occupancy requirements are met.

Eligible non-borrowing spouse

HUD rules may allow certain non-borrowing spouses to remain in the home after the borrower dies or permanently leaves for health reasons if all applicable conditions are satisfied.

- Eligibility is rule-specific and should be documented at origination.
- Marriage and principal-residence requirements matter.
- Do not assume that every spouse who is not on the loan will automatically be protected.

FAMILY DOCUMENTATION

Before closing, ask the counselor, lender, and estate-planning attorney to explain in writing what happens if either spouse dies first, moves to long-term care, divorces, or changes title.

Official source note: HUD HECM program materials; HUD housing-counseling guidance; and CFPB reverse-mortgage consumer guidance. Verify current rules and limits.

HEIRS & REPAYMENT

Heirs, Repayment & Non-Recourse Protection

The home can still pass to heirs, but the HECM must be resolved when it becomes due and payable.

If heirs want to sell

The home can be sold and the HECM repaid from sale proceeds. If the sale produces more than the amount owed and transaction costs, the remaining equity belongs to the estate or owners.

If heirs want to keep the home

Heirs may need cash or new financing to satisfy the HECM. CFPB notes that when the balance exceeds the home value, HECM rules can permit payoff based on 95% of the current appraised value in specified circumstances. Obtain current servicing instructions.

Non-recourse does not mean no repayment

The FHA insurance structure protects against personal liability beyond applicable collateral rules, but the home remains the security for the debt.

Time matters after a death

Servicers issue due-and-payable notices and deadlines. Families should contact the servicer promptly and document efforts to sell, refinance, or otherwise resolve the loan.

LEGACY PLAN

A legacy strategy is stronger when heirs know the estimated balance, expected home value, who wants the property, how a payoff could be financed, and who will communicate with the servicer.

Official source note: HUD HECM program materials; HUD housing-counseling guidance; and CFPB reverse-mortgage consumer guidance. Verify current rules and limits.

ESTATE COORDINATION

Estate Planning: What a HECM Does Not Replace

Mortgage planning and estate planning intersect, but they solve different problems.

HECM questions

- How much is borrowed and when?
- What property obligations continue?
- When does the loan become due?
- What payment or credit options are available?
- How might the balance affect remaining home equity?

Estate questions

- Who owns the property and how is title held?
- Who inherits under a will, trust, deed, or state law?
- Who has authority under powers of attorney?
- What happens if capacity declines?
- How will heirs fund, sell, or decline the property?

DO NOT PACKAGE THE DECISIONS

A mortgage professional should not provide legal or tax conclusions outside their role. Use independent estate-planning and tax professionals for title, trust, probate, beneficiary, and tax questions.

Official source note: HUD HECM program materials; HUD housing-counseling guidance; and CFPB reverse-mortgage consumer guidance. Verify current rules and limits.

FIT TEST

When a HECM May Fit

Suitability depends on the household objective, expected occupancy, budget, and alternatives.

Characteristics that can support a fit

- The homeowner expects to remain in the property for a meaningful period and the home is suitable for aging in place.
- The monthly mortgage payment or lack of liquidity creates retirement pressure that a HECM could address.
- The household can reliably sustain taxes, insurance, maintenance, association charges, and normal living costs.
- The draw strategy is limited to documented needs rather than maximum borrowing capacity.

Planning conditions

- The family understands that the balance may grow and future equity may decline.
- Spouse and heir expectations are discussed before closing.
- Alternatives have been compared on cost, risk, flexibility, and housing suitability.
- Counseling, lender estimates, and professional reviews are consistent enough to support an informed decision.

NO UNIVERSAL "BEST"

A HECM can be useful in the right plan and harmful in the wrong one. The goal is not to prove that reverse mortgages are good or bad; it is to determine whether this specific household can defend the decision.

Official source note: HUD HECM program materials; HUD housing-counseling guidance; and CFPB reverse-mortgage consumer guidance. Verify current rules and limits.

NO-FIT TEST

When a HECM May Not Fit

A strong decision process identifies reasons to stop as clearly as reasons to proceed.

Potential stop signs

- The homeowner expects to move soon or the home no longer fits health, accessibility, family, or maintenance needs.
- Property taxes, insurance, repairs, or association costs are already unsustainable.
- The household needs a very large amount of cash but the HECM would provide only limited net proceeds after required payoffs.
- A family member or third party is pressuring the homeowner to borrow for someone else's benefit.

Alternatives may be stronger when

- Downsizing releases more usable equity and lowers recurring housing costs.
- A lower-cost home equity product is affordable and the borrower can reliably make monthly payments.
- Public assistance, property-tax relief, repair grants, budget reductions, or family support solve the problem without adding mortgage debt.
- Waiting improves the household's position or clarifies a near-term housing transition.

WALK-AWAY STANDARD

If the plan requires optimistic home appreciation, perfect health, no repair surprises, and repeated future draws simply to stay afloat, pause. A retirement strategy should remain workable under ordinary stress.

Official source note: HUD HECM program materials; HUD housing-counseling guidance; and CFPB reverse-mortgage consumer guidance. Verify current rules and limits.

PART II

Retirement Strategy & Implementation

This section presents a cohesive case study showing how retirement goals, cash flow, property, family legacy, insurance, and professional responsibilities must be evaluated together.

Important Disclosures

- This case study is fictional / generalized and is for education.
- It does not determine HECM qualification, guaranteed proceeds, or recommend a lender or insurer.
- HECM terms, costs, rates, financial assessment, and property requirements must be verified by an FHA-approved lender and an independent HUD-approved counselor.
- Life insurance is not guaranteed to repay a future loan balance; it is only a potential repayment resource and depends on underwriting, carrier approval, policy terms, premiums, and lapse risk.
- Organization- or church-related property transfers can create legal, tax, fiduciary, title, compensation, donor-restriction, and governance consequences.
- The workbook uses simplified assumptions that must be replaced by verified written information before making decisions.
- No governmental endorsement.

How to Use This Section

1. Review the fictional case profile and identify the planning path that resembles your situation.
2. Complete the household income and expense workbook entries.
3. Gather title, lien, property-charge, appraisal, and estate information.
4. Complete independent HUD-approved HECM counseling before treating a reverse mortgage as a final option.
5. Obtain written lender estimates and separate insurance illustrations.
6. Compare the original concept with the redesigned strategy, alternatives, and annual review process.

WORKBOOK CONNECTION: The workbook is the calculation engine; this section is the decision and implementation roadmap.

The Heritage Household

Case Profile & Planning Paths

Case Profile At-A-Glance

Household	Married retirement-age homeowners; younger relevant age must be verified.
Property	Principal residence or property proposed to become the retiree's principal residence.
Illustrative Property Value	$450,000
Original Cash Target	$300,000 reverse-mortgage proceeds
Original Insurance Concept	$750,000 fixed death benefit, 20-year term initially considered
Retirement Cash Flow	$4,100 monthly income $5,300 monthly expenses
Budget Gap	$1,200 per month
Legacy Goal	Preserve a realistic opportunity for heirs to retain the home.
Planning Concern	Loan growth, premium duration, property obligations, and long-term affordability.

Why This Case Matters

A home is more than an asset—it is a centerpiece of retirement security and family legacy. The mortgage, household budget, policy guarantees, ownership, beneficiaries, and estate plan must all be analyzed together to create a responsible, sustainable strategy.

Path A — Existing Personal Residence

1. Confirm title and spouse rights.
2. Confirm principal residence.
3. Complete budget and ongoing charges.
4. Complete HUD-approved counseling.
5. Obtain written lender estimates using the youngest relevant age, expected rate, and property value.
6. Choose a draw structure that matches the need.
7. Underwrite insurance separately.
8. Coordinate the beneficiary, estate, and heir payoff plan; review the plan annually.

Path B — Organization-Conveyed Residence

1. Review deed, bylaws, donor restrictions, and authority to convey.
2. Obtain an independent appraisal.
3. Have disinterested decision-makers review compensation and recuse the intended recipient.
4. Review legal, tax, and title consequences.
5. Execute and record the deed.
6. Establish ownership and occupancy.
7. Only then pursue a formal HECM through an independent lender.

Sequence Matters

A promise to transfer property is not the same as completed ownership. Timing and order directly affect eligibility and outcomes.

PART II

From Concept to a Defensible Plan

Case Redesign, Goals & Cash Flow

Original Concept vs. Redesigned Approach

Original Concept	Redesigned Approach
☒ Assumed $300,000 proceeds →	✓ Use lender-determined feasibility; do not promise a target amount.
☒ Large immediate lump sum →	✓ Evaluate limited draw, line of credit, tenure, or term payments.
☒ $750,000 20-year term policy →	✓ Underwrite long-duration coverage or a reserve and stress-test advanced ages.
☒ Insurance "indemnifies" the loan →	✓ Benefit only as a repayment resource controlled by the beneficiary or trust.
☒ Mortgage and insurance packaged together →	✓ Use independent lender, counselor, and insurance professional; no required cross-sale.
☒ Informal church support →	✓ Use written compensation terms, appraisal, recusal, comparability data, and separate approval.
☒ Home automatically remains with heirs →	✓ Create a documented payoff, refinance, sale, and estate-administration plan.
☒ One-time approval →	✓ Use staged due diligence, final approval, closing, and annual monitoring.

Central Principle

Build the plan around the smallest sustainable amount that accomplishes the retirement objective, not the maximum amount that can be borrowed.

1 Define the Retirement & Legacy Goals

- What is the monthly income need?
- Is a large lump sum really necessary?
- How long does the homeowner expect to remain in the home?
- Does a spouse intend to remain?
- Is home retention a firm legacy goal?
- What reserves should remain outside the loan?
- What alternatives have already been considered?

2 Build the Household Cash-Flow Picture

Monthly income does not directly establish the HECM principal limit but strongly affects financial assessment and future draws.

Monthly Income		Monthly Expenses		Monthly Gap
$4,100	−	$5,300	=	$1,200

- Income is $1,200 less than expenses each month.
- The reverse mortgage is designed to help close this gap while supporting retirement and legacy goals.

STEPS 3–5

Verify the Property, Eligibility & Assessment

These steps ensure the property is suitable, the borrower meets requirements, and the plan is financially sustainable before proceeding.

3 Verify Property, Title and Ongoing Charges

- Gather the deed and all title documents.
- Confirm ownership form, spouse rights, and any existing liens or encumbrances.
- Verify that the property is the borrower's principal residence.
- Gather property taxes, homeowners insurance, flood insurance (if applicable), HOA assessments, and maintenance obligations.
- Understand that title or lien problems can delay or derail the plan.

5 Understand the Financial Assessment

- The lender evaluates how the borrower will continue paying taxes, insurance, and ongoing property obligations.
- Income, residual cash flow, credit history, and the ability to pay property charges are key factors.
- If the file is weak, the lender may require a set-aside for future property charges.

4 Complete Counseling and Confirm HECM Eligibility

- Independent HUD-approved counseling is a consumer-protection step—not a sales presentation.
- HECM availability is generally influenced by the youngest borrower or eligible non-borrowing spouse, expected interest rates, and the property value.
- The counseling certificate does not guarantee loan approval.
- Borrowers still need lender underwriting to qualify.

Why These Steps Matter

Thorough verification protects both the borrower and the lender. The property is not only the source of your equity—it is also the collateral securing the loan. Getting these details right helps ensure a strong, sustainable plan.

WORKBOOK CONNECTION: Use the companion workbook to collect documents, run your financial assessment, and prepare for counseling.

STEPS 6–8

Written Estimates, Draw Strategy & Insurance

These final steps help you compare written terms, match the right draw approach to your needs, and evaluate insurance independently.

6 Obtain Written Lender Feasibility Estimates

Request itemized, written terms—not a verbal proceeds estimate.

Request These Written Terms
✓ Expected rate / margin / index
✓ Principal limit estimate
✓ Mandatory obligations
✓ Closing costs
✓ Mortgage insurance premiums
✓ Servicing fees, if any
✓ Draw options and related fees
✓ Projected remaining availability

Base your decision on itemized written terms, not a verbal proceeds estimate.

7 Choose a Draw Strategy That Fits the Need

Different approaches offer different flexibility, costs, and long-term impact.

Draw Strategy	Best Used For
Limited Initial Draw	Start with smaller needs and preserve availability.
Line of Credit	Maximum flexibility and protection against volatility.
Tenure Payments	Steady payments for as long as you live in the home.
Term Payments	Payments for a set number of years.
Lump Sum (Use Cautiously)	Reserved for clearly defined, essential needs.

The payment structure can matter as much as the headline proceeds amount.

8 Underwrite Life Insurance Separately

- Insurance can support a legacy plan, but it cannot be assumed to match an unknown future loan balance.
- Federal law prohibits conditioning HECM eligibility on the purchase of insurance.
- Insurance must be evaluated independently for:

Underwriting Requirements	Guarantee Strength	Affordability & Premium Duration	Beneficiary Design	Lapse Risk

Important Notice

Do not package the mortgage and insurance as a single, assumed solution.

Evaluate the loan and insurance separately and on their own merits.

STEPS 9–10 & PROFESSIONAL INTEGRATION

Heir Retention, Governance & the Professional Team

9 Create the Estate and Heir Retention Plan

- Non-recourse protection limits exposure to the home's value, but it does not automatically allow heirs to keep the home.
- Heirs who want to retain the home generally need a realistic payoff, refinance, or sale plan based on future cash flow.
- Coordinate title, spouse protections, wills, trusts, powers of attorney, beneficiary choices, and contingency planning.

10 Use Independent Governance for Organization Benefits

- Property transfer or church-paid insurance can be compensation—but it must be reasonable, documented, and approved without conflicted control.
- Use appraisal, comparability data, and recusal to ensure conflicts are avoided.
- Document decisions, obtain legal review, report taxes, and secure separate final approval.

Build One Coordinated Team Without Cross-Selling

- **HUD-approved counselor:** Alternatives, costs, obligations, and counseling certificate.
- **FHA-approved HECM lender:** Eligibility review, written estimates, appraisal, costs, and loan terms.
- **Insurance professional:** Separate underwriting, guarantees, premiums, beneficiaries, lapse risk, and carrier strength.
- **Estate-planning attorney:** Title, spouse and heir protections, trusts, powers, probate, and payoff planning.
- **Tax professional:** Compensation, benefits, transfer, deduction, and reporting questions.
- **Financial professional:** Cash flow, reserves, investments, longevity, alternatives, and scenario testing.

COORDINATION NOTE: Each professional must have an independent role and act in the best interest of the homeowner. The process should be transparent, well-documented, and free from cross-selling pressure.

PART II

Illustrative Analysis & Stress Testing

Projections, Equity, and Budget Pressure

1 Projection Assumptions and Milestones

The numbers below are illustrative only and for education. They are not a quote or commitment from any lender. Actual results will vary.

Category	What It Represents	Illustrative Example
Starting HECM Balance (Including Financed Costs)	Initial principal limit plus financed up-front costs and fees.	$215,400
Projected Interest & Mortgage-Insurance Accrual	Interest and insurance charges that accrue each month.	~5.00% (Illustrative APR)*
Illustrative Property Value Growth	Potential annual change in home value.	3.0% annually (Illustrative)
Example Fixed Death Benefit	HECM fixed repayment limit due at maturity.	$450,000 (Illustrative)

**Includes estimated interest rate and mortgage insurance premium; actual rates will vary.*

2 Balance, Property Value and Fixed Death Benefit

- The loan balance can grow over time.
- The property value may also change.
- The fixed death benefit may not keep pace with a growing payoff.
- The gap between the loan balance and the fixed benefit can widen.

Conceptual Illustration Over Time

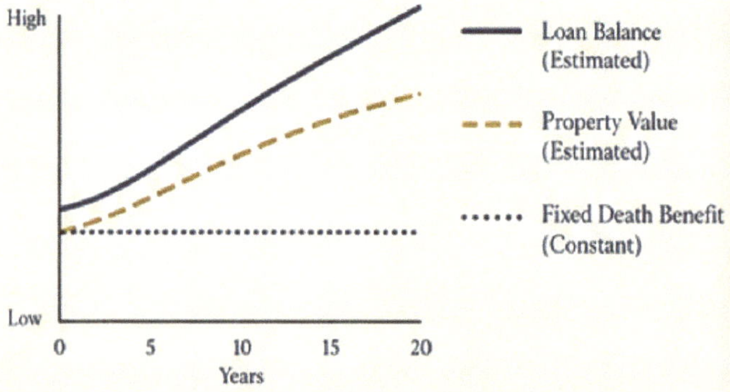

3 How a Budget Deficit Changes the Legacy Plan

- Repeatedly using home-equity draws to cover a budget deficit increases the loan balance.
- A persistent monthly gap can accelerate interest and insurance accrual.
- Rising costs for taxes, insurance, and maintenance can reduce net equity over time.
- A larger balance at maturity can affect your heirs' options, including their ability to keep the home.

Key Takeaway

Stress-test the plan, not just the initial illustration. Run the numbers under different scenarios so you can make informed decisions today—and be prepared tomorrow.

PART II

Repayment Resources, Alternatives & Timeline

Compare the Plan Before You Commit

1. Potential Repayment Resources

Resource	Strengths	Risks / Considerations
Life Insurance	Potential to provide sum needed at death.	May be costly or unavailable; death benefit reduced by existing loans.
Sale or Refinance of the Property	Can pay off loan in full; creates liquidity.	May require moving; market timing risk; transaction costs.
Savings or Dedicated Reserves	Does not reduce estate; immediate access.	May be insufficient; erodes emergency reserves.
Family Support or Shared Housing	Reduces cash need; strengthens family relationships.	Dependent on long-term willingness and ability; potential family tension.
Organization-Based Reserves or Retirement Funding	Aligns with mission; can provide stability and scale.	Policy limits, donor restrictions, or market volatility may apply.

2. Compare the HECM Plan With Other Paths

- **Downsize or Sell and Relocate** – Unlocks equity by selling and moving to a lower-cost residence.
- **Traditional Home-Equity Loan or Refinance** – Borrow with fixed payments; preserves full equity if repaid.
- **Property-Tax Relief or Public Benefits** – Reduce ongoing costs through exemptions, deferrals, or assistance programs.
- **Family Support or Shared Housing** – Share expenses or living space to reduce cash needs.
- **Organization Retains Residence and Provides Stipend/ Lease Support** – Keep the home while the organization provides ongoing support or a lease arrangement.
- **Preserving Home Equity With No HECM** – Continue saving, investing, or using other resources without a reverse mortgage.

Decision Rule: Reject the HECM structure when a less complex option achieves the objective with lower risk or stronger long-term sustainability.

3. A 90-Day Due-Diligence Timeline

Days 1–15
- Clarify goals and success metrics.
- Complete the household workbook.
- Organize the property file.
- Review authority and decision rights.

Days 16–30
- Complete HUD-approved counseling.
- Review title status and liens.
- Plan appraisal and inspections.
- Begin initial lender conversations.

Days 31–45
- Gather written HECM estimates.
- Obtain insurance applications and quotes.
- Compare alternative strategies and resource options.

Days 46–60
- Integrate legal review (estate, liens, authority).
- Review tax impacts and reporting.
- Confirm governance and policy compliance.

Days 61–75
- Run final stress test of cash flow and obligations.
- Hold heir/family conference.
- Develop contingency and repayment plan.

Days 76–90
- Finalize household or organizational decision.
- Prepare closing documents if approved.
- Confirm post-closing monitoring plan.

4. Stop Points

Pause if any of the following apply:

- Title is unclear or unresolved liens exist.
- Budget remains structurally negative.
- Insurance is unavailable or unaffordable.
- Heirs lack a realistic payoff plan.
- Professionals identify unresolved legal, tax, or fiduciary risk.

PART II

Meeting Tools, Readiness & Ongoing Management

From Feasibility Review to Annual Follow-Up

These tools help families and leaders conduct productive meetings, make informed decisions, and manage the reverse mortgage responsibly for years to come.

Suggested Feasibility Meeting Agenda

1. Opening purpose and conflict disclosures.
2. Retirement objective and cash-flow review.
3. Property ownership, appraisal, liens and charges.
4. HUD counseling and written HECM estimates.
5. Draw-strategy comparison and projected balances.
6. Insurance underwriting status.
7. Estate and heir plan.
8. Legal, tax, compensation and governance findings.
9. Alternatives reviewed.
10. Final decision options.

Sample Feasibility Motion

I move that we:

- Authorize an independent feasibility study of a HECM as one potential solution.
- Allow appraisal and due-diligence work, including counseling and written estimates.
- Acknowledge that no deed or long-term premium obligation is approved at this time.
- Require that the intended recipient(s) recuse from all discussions and votes.
- Require a separate final approval meeting before any implementation.

Ongoing Management & Annual Review

- Deed and title remain in good standing.
- Loan disclosures and amortization schedules on file.
- Insurance policy active and adequate.
- Estate documents current.
- Organization minutes and approvals maintained.
- Annual property-taxes and insurance proof on file.
- Current HECM balance and available borrowing capacity.
- Remaining line of credit or term availability.
- Property value changes and market conditions.
- Insurance affordability and underwriting status.
- Health, occupancy, and care needs changes.
- Heir intentions and estate plan updates.

Decision Scorecard

Score each factor: 0 = Weak 1 = Moderate 2 = Strong

1	Cash-flow sustainability	0	1	2
2	Property-charge capacity	0	1	2
3	Insurance or reserve fit	0	1	2
4	Heir retention plan	0	1	2
5	Legal/title/tax review	0	1	2
6	Governance/conflicts	0	1	2

Master Readiness & Due-Diligence Checklist

Planning Foundations
- ☐ Written retirement goals and priorities
- ☐ Completed Household Income & Expense Workbook

Property & Title
- ☐ Deed and title ownership verified
- ☐ Liens, judgments, and encumbrances reviewed

Taxes & Insurance
- ☐ Property taxes current or escrow plan in place
- ☐ Homeowners insurance in force and adequate

HECM Requirements
- ☐ HUD-approved counseling certificate obtained
- ☐ Written lender estimates and disclosures received
- ☐ Payment-plan options compared in writing
- ☐ Insurance underwriting and eligibility confirmed

Estate & Family
- ☐ Beneficiaries and estate documents reviewed
- ☐ Heir intentions and retention plan discussed

Analysis & Oversight
- ☐ Alternative strategies compared
- ☐ Conflict-of-interest disclosures completed
- ☐ Reasonable comparability analysis completed

Governance & Documentation
- ☐ Written agreements and policies in place
- ☐ Annual review date assigned and recorded

Important Interpretation

A low score does not mean "borrow more." It means pause, gather information, revise the structure, or choose an alternative.

COORDINATION CHECKLIST

Build the Right Professional Team

No single professional should be expected to answer every mortgage, tax, legal, insurance, estate, and household-planning question.

1. ## HUD-approved housing counselor

   Independent education, alternatives, costs, obligations, and counseling certificate.

2. ## FHA-approved HECM lender

   Current eligibility review, written estimates, financial assessment, appraisal, costs, and loan terms.

3. ## Estate-planning attorney

   Title, spouse and heir protections, trusts, powers of attorney, probate, and payoff planning.

4. ## Tax professional

   Tax treatment, property transfer, compensation, benefits, deductions, and reporting questions.

5. ## Insurance professional

   Separate underwriting, guarantees, premium duration, beneficiaries, lapse risk, and carrier strength.

6. ## Financial professional

   Cash flow, reserves, investments, longevity, retirement income, alternatives, and scenario testing.

MEETING STANDARD

Ask for written figures, note the date and source of each answer, disclose relevant conflicts, and do not sign until the documents match what you understand.

Official source note: HUD HECM program materials; HUD housing-counseling guidance; and CFPB reverse-mortgage consumer guidance. Verify current rules and limits.

PART II - ALTERNATIVES

Alternative Strategies Before Borrowing

Compare the HECM with real alternatives using the same household facts.

A reverse mortgage should not be evaluated against “do nothing” only. Build at least three realistic alternatives and compare the monthly effect, one-time costs, housing stability, flexibility, and legacy consequences.

Alternative	Potential strength	Potential tradeoff
Downsize and buy with cash	Can lower carrying costs and release equity.	Moving cost, emotional disruption, transaction costs.
Traditional refinance	May lower payment without reverse-mortgage structure.	Income/credit qualification and required monthly payments.
HELOC / home equity loan	May have lower upfront costs for modest needs.	Required monthly payments; variable-rate risk may apply.
Budget / assistance / tax relief	May solve a smaller gap without new mortgage debt.	May not address a large existing mortgage or capital need.
HECM	Can remove required monthly principal-and-interest payment and create flexible access.	Growing balance, fees, property obligations, reduced future equity.

COMPARE LIKE WITH LIKE

Use the same five-year or ten-year horizon for every option. Include housing costs, financing costs, moving costs, maintenance, taxes, insurance, and realistic family goals.

Official source note: HUD HECM program materials; HUD housing-counseling guidance; and CFPB reverse-mortgage consumer guidance. Verify current rules and limits.

PART II - ILLUSTRATIVE CASE STUDY

Case Study A: Cash-Flow Relief

Fictional numbers for education only; obtain current written estimates before making a decision.

Marian - Age 72 - Wants to Remain in Her Home

Home value	$430,000 illustrative
Current mortgage	$82,000; $1,050 monthly P&I
Monthly income	$3,850
Property charges	$620 monthly average
Emergency cash	$18,000
Primary goal	Reduce fixed monthly pressure without moving

Questions to test

- After the existing mortgage is paid off, how much usable HECM capacity remains?
- Can Marian still afford taxes, insurance, repairs, healthcare, and food without future borrowing?
- Would a smaller line of credit plus targeted draws preserve more equity than taking cash immediately?
- What does the five- and ten-year projected balance look like?

Planning analysis

The existing mortgage payment is a meaningful share of monthly income, so removing that required payment could materially improve cash flow.

Because Marian wants to stay in the home, property condition and maintenance reserves are as important as the mortgage calculation.

The strongest structure may be the one that uses the least immediate borrowing while keeping an emergency reserve available.

CASE TAKEAWAY

The case may support continued HECM due diligence, but only after written estimates show enough net proceeds, a sustainable post-closing budget, and a documented repair reserve.

Official source note: HUD HECM program materials; HUD housing-counseling guidance; and CFPB reverse-mortgage consumer guidance. Verify current rules and limits.

CASE A - DECISION ANALYSIS

Why Cash-Flow Relief Is Not the Whole Answer

A lower monthly obligation improves the budget only if the rest of the housing plan remains sustainable.

Measure the payment actually removed

Separate principal and interest from taxes and insurance if the current mortgage payment includes escrow. HECM does not erase taxes, insurance, maintenance, or association charges.

Reserve for the house

A 72-year-old homeowner may face roof, HVAC, plumbing, accessibility, or insurance-cost shocks. A plan that spends all available proceeds at closing can leave the borrower house-rich and cash-poor again.

Use a stress case

Reduce income by 10%, increase property charges by 15%, and add a major repair. Does the household still have a credible plan?

Define success

Success is not “the loan closed.” Success is that Marian can remain safely housed, meet obligations, preserve emergency liquidity, and understand the effect on heirs.

DECISION GATE

Proceed only if the written plan solves more risk than it creates. If the post-closing budget remains fragile, compare downsizing or other housing changes before closing.

Official source note: HUD HECM program materials; HUD housing-counseling guidance; and CFPB reverse-mortgage consumer guidance. Verify current rules and limits.

PART II - ILLUSTRATIVE CASE STUDY

Case Study B: Downsizing May Be Stronger

Fictional numbers for education only; obtain current written estimates before making a decision.

Robert and Elena - Ages 68 and 66 - Large Home, Shorter Time Horizon

Home value	$560,000 illustrative
Current mortgage	$235,000
Monthly income	$5,700
Home condition	Roof and HVAC likely within 5 years
Expected move	Possibly 3-4 years
Primary goal	Lower housing burden before health needs increase

Questions to test

- How much HECM capacity remains after paying off the current mortgage?
- Would large repairs consume much of the available benefit?
- If they move in three years, are the closing costs justified?
- What would selling and purchasing a smaller home do to monthly costs and liquid reserves?

Planning analysis

A shorter expected occupancy period can make high transaction costs harder to justify.

The current home may be too expensive to maintain even if the mortgage payment disappears.

Downsizing could address mortgage debt, taxes, maintenance, accessibility, and future care logistics at the same time.

CASE TAKEAWAY

A HECM is not automatically the best way to age in place. If the home itself is becoming the problem, changing the housing asset may solve more than changing the financing.

Official source note: HUD HECM program materials; HUD housing-counseling guidance; and CFPB reverse-mortgage consumer guidance. Verify current rules and limits.

CASE B - DECISION ANALYSIS

When the House - Not the Mortgage - Is the Problem

Financing should not lock a household into a property that no longer supports retirement.

Time horizon matters

Closing costs have more time to be absorbed when the borrower expects to stay longer. A likely move in three or four years deserves careful cost comparison.

Maintenance is part of affordability

A large home with major deferred maintenance can remain expensive even without a monthly mortgage payment.

Accessibility can outweigh sentiment

Stairs, bathroom layout, distance to medical care, yard work, and driving demands can become retirement costs.

Compare net housing wealth after the move

Estimate sale proceeds, transaction costs, new-home purchase price, recurring costs, and the emergency reserve remaining after relocation.

NO-SUNK-COST THINKING

The years already spent in a home do not require the household to remain there. Evaluate the next ten years based on safety, affordability, support, and quality of life.

Official source note: HUD HECM program materials; HUD housing-counseling guidance; and CFPB reverse-mortgage consumer guidance. Verify current rules and limits.

PART II - ILLUSTRATIVE CASE STUDY

Case Study C: Standby Liquidity

Fictional numbers for education only; obtain current written estimates before making a decision.

James and Lorraine - Ages 74 and 72 - Mortgage-Free, Strong Cash Flow

Home value	$710,000 illustrative
Current mortgage	$0
Monthly income	$7,400
Investments	Moderate retirement portfolio
Emergency cash	$55,000
	Create a backup source of liquidity in a downturn

Questions to test

- Is a HECM line of credit worth the upfront cost if it is rarely used?
- How much liquidity already exists outside the home?
- Would a conventional HELOC be available and more economical?
- What spending rules will prevent the line from becoming routine income?

Planning analysis

The household does not need a HECM to survive monthly expenses, so the decision is primarily about optionality and liquidity.

A standby line can be evaluated as one component of a broader retirement plan, but the upfront and ongoing costs must be weighed against the probability of use.

The couple should compare HECM, HELOC, cash reserves, portfolio withdrawals, and downsizing before selecting a tool.

CASE TAKEAWAY

A HECM can be evaluated as a strategic reserve, but "available credit" should not be confused with wealth creation. The value depends on flexibility, cost, and disciplined use.

Official source note: HUD HECM program materials; HUD housing-counseling guidance; and CFPB reverse-mortgage consumer guidance. Verify current rules and limits.

CASE C - DECISION ANALYSIS

Liquidity Is Valuable Only When It Solves a Defined Risk

A standby resource can reduce pressure, but every financing tool has a carrying cost or opportunity cost.

Identify the risk being insured

Is the concern a market downturn, long-term care expense, major home repair, or temporary cash-flow disruption? Different risks may call for different resources.

Build a draw order

Write the order in which cash, insurance benefits, portfolio withdrawals, family support, or home equity would be used. A HECM line should have a defined place in that order.

Compare access reliability

A HELOC can have different underwriting and availability characteristics than a HECM line of credit. Ask what could cause each facility to change, freeze, or become unavailable.

Review annually

A strategy that makes sense at 74 may not be the best strategy at 82. Update balances, health needs, property condition, and family intentions.

STRATEGIC DISCIPLINE

The purpose of standby liquidity is to reduce forced decisions during stress. It should not become permission to increase routine spending without regard to the growing loan balance.

Official source note: HUD HECM program materials; HUD housing-counseling guidance; and CFPB reverse-mortgage consumer guidance. Verify current rules and limits.

FAMILY GOVERNANCE

The Family Decision Meeting

A structured conversation can prevent misunderstandings that surface years after closing.

Explain the objective first

Start with the retirement problem the household is trying to solve. Family members can evaluate the strategy more fairly when they understand the goal rather than seeing only the loan amount.

Separate decision rights from opinions

The homeowner retains decision authority. Adult children and other relatives can ask questions and help with planning, but should not pressure the borrower toward a result that benefits them.

Discuss the home honestly

Ask who actually wants the home, who could realistically afford a future payoff, and whether retaining the property is a true family goal or an assumption.

Document the plan

Record the lender/servicer contact, estate representative, key documents, estimated balance, and intended first steps after death, incapacity, or a move.

SUGGESTED OPENING

"We are not meeting to vote on my house. We are meeting so everyone understands the plan, the risks, and what each person should do if something happens to me."

Official source note: HUD HECM program materials; HUD housing-counseling guidance; and CFPB reverse-mortgage consumer guidance. Verify current rules and limits.

HEIR RETENTION

Heir-Retention Funding Map

A wish to keep the home becomes a plan only when the family identifies a realistic payoff resource.

When a HECM becomes due, heirs who want to retain the property generally need another source of funds or financing. Build the retention plan before closing and update it over time.

Potential resource	Strength	Question to verify
Cash / estate liquidity	Fast and simple if sufficient.	Will enough liquid cash remain after final expenses and other obligations?
Heir mortgage / refinance	Preserves the property if the heir qualifies.	Who would borrow, and is future qualification realistic?
Life-insurance proceeds	Can create designated liquidity if coverage remains in force.	Is the policy affordable, underwritten, owned correctly, and sufficient?
Sale of other assets	May provide payoff funds.	Would liquidation create tax, timing, or family conflicts?
Sell the home	Repays HECM and distributes remaining equity.	Who has authority, and how quickly can the sale process begin?

NO GUARANTEE LANGUAGE

Do not say life insurance "pays off the reverse mortgage" unless a policy is actually issued, remains in force, and proceeds are available when needed. Treat insurance as a separate risk-management decision.

Official source note: HUD HECM program materials; HUD housing-counseling guidance; and CFPB reverse-mortgage consumer guidance. Verify current rules and limits.

INSURANCE COORDINATION

Separate Decision, Separate Underwriting

Life insurance may support a legacy objective, but it should never be presented as an automatic companion to a HECM.

Mortgage decision

- Evaluates home equity, housing goals, cash flow, property obligations, and borrowing terms.
- Requires HECM counseling and lender underwriting.
- Should stand on its own merits even if no insurance policy is purchased.

Insurance decision

- Depends on age, health, underwriting, premium affordability, policy type, guarantees, and carrier strength.
- Requires a licensed insurance professional and policy-specific illustration.
- Should be stress-tested for premium duration, lapse risk, beneficiary design, and long-term affordability.

CONFLICT CONTROL
When the same person or organization can benefit financially from multiple products, disclose compensation and roles clearly. Independent review is especially valuable when mortgage, insurance, estate, or investment decisions intersect.

Official source note: HUD HECM program materials; HUD housing-counseling guidance; and CFPB reverse-mortgage consumer guidance. Verify current rules and limits.

CONSUMER PROTECTION

Pressure Tactics & Red Flags

A strong decision process protects the homeowner from urgency, confusion, and third-party agendas.

Slow down if you hear

- "You need to sign today before the program disappears."
- "The bank will own your home anyway."
- "You can never lose the house."
- "Take the maximum cash now - you can invest the difference."
- "Your children will not need to do anything later."

Protect the decision

- Complete independent HUD-approved counseling.
- Compare written estimates from more than one lender when practical.
- Verify licenses, company identity, fees, and complaint channels.
- Never sign blank documents or transfer title to obtain a loan.
- Keep copies of every disclosure, estimate, appraisal, counseling certificate, and closing document.

RIGHT TO CANCEL
Most HECM refinance transactions include a federal three-business-day right of rescission after closing; HECM for Purchase transactions are treated differently. Ask the lender and closing professional which cancellation rights apply to the exact transaction.

Official source note: HUD HECM program materials; HUD housing-counseling guidance; and CFPB reverse-mortgage consumer guidance. Verify current rules and limits.

LENDER COMPARISON

The 10-Question Lender Comparison

Make every lender answer the same questions so the household can compare substance rather than presentation.

Record the date, loan type, rate structure, and source of every answer. If one answer changes, ask for an updated written illustration.

#	Question	Why it matters
1	What gross and net proceeds are available?	Separates headline amount from usable funds.
2	What mandatory obligations are paid at closing?	Shows how much capacity is consumed immediately.
3	What are all upfront costs?	Supports lender-to-lender comparison.
4	What rate structure applies?	Affects future balance and flexibility.
5	What payment plans are available?	Determines access to funds.
6	Is a LESA required?	Can materially reduce free proceeds.
7	What is the five-, ten-, and fifteen-year projected balance?	Makes long-term cost visible.
8	What happens if we sell or move?	Clarifies exit mechanics.
9	How is a spouse treated?	Protects occupancy planning.
10	Who services the loan and how do we get help?	Sets expectations after closing.

WRITE IT DOWN

Do not choose a lender because one estimate shows more cash. Ask why the numbers differ and whether the difference comes from rates, margins, fees, assumptions, property value, or loan structure.

Official source note: HUD HECM program materials; HUD housing-counseling guidance; and CFPB reverse-mortgage consumer guidance. Verify current rules and limits.

ANNUAL REVIEW

Annual HECM Review Dashboard

The loan is a long-term housing arrangement; the plan should be reviewed at least once each year.

Housing status

Confirm principal-residence occupancy, property condition, expected repairs, taxes, insurance, association charges, and any notices from the servicer.

Loan status

Record current HECM balance, available line of credit or remaining payment-plan capacity, current rate information, and any recent draws.

Household status

Update income, recurring expenses, health needs, emergency reserves, caregiver arrangements, and expected time in the home.

Family and estate status

Confirm spouse status, beneficiaries, estate documents, powers of attorney, trusted contacts, and whether heirs still intend to retain or sell the home.

Decision trigger

Define events that require a new professional review - large repair, death of spouse, health-care move, insurance cancellation, property-tax increase, or major draw request.

REVIEW RULE

A HECM should not become “set it and forget it.” The safest plan is one the household can explain, monitor, and update as circumstances change.

Official source note: HUD HECM program materials; HUD housing-counseling guidance; and CFPB reverse-mortgage consumer guidance. Verify current rules and limits.

PRE-CLOSING GATE

Pre-Closing Decision Gate

Before signing, every major question should have an owner, a source, and a written answer.

Loan terms verified
Current lender estimate reviewed; rate structure, proceeds, costs, mandatory obligations, payment plan, and projected balances understood.

Property plan verified
Taxes, insurance, maintenance reserve, association charges, repair needs, and occupancy plan are sustainable.

Spouse and heir plan verified
Borrower/co-borrower/non-borrowing-spouse status is understood; estate and heir-retention strategy has been discussed with appropriate professionals.

Alternatives documented
At least two reasonable alternatives have been considered and the reasons for accepting or rejecting them are written down.

No unresolved pressure
The borrower understands the transaction, is not being rushed, and can describe the purpose of the loan and the consequences in plain language.

FINAL QUESTION

If the lender called tomorrow and said the HECM was unavailable, what would the household do instead? If there is no answer, the plan may still be too dependent on one product.

Official source note: HUD HECM program materials; HUD housing-counseling guidance; and CFPB reverse-mortgage consumer guidance. Verify current rules and limits.

REFERENCE

Glossary and Official Source Notes

PLAIN-LANGUAGE TERMS

HECM	FHA-insured Home Equity Conversion Mortgage.
PRINCIPAL LIMIT	Maximum loan capacity before deductions and restrictions.
MCA	Maximum claim amount used within program calculations.
LESA	Funds reserved for certain property charges after financial assessment.
ELIGIBLE NON-BORROWING SPOUSE	A spouse who may receive specified protections when HUD requirements are met.
NON-RECOURSE	Borrower or heirs generally are not personally liable beyond applicable collateral rules.
POLICY ILLUSTRATION	Life-insurance projection showing guaranteed and non-guaranteed elements.
EXCESS BENEFIT	Economic benefit above reasonable value in certain tax-exempt organization transactions.

CURRENT PRIMARY SOURCES

[1] **HUD - FHA Reverse Mortgage for Seniors** — hud.gov/hud-partners/single-family-hecmhome
[2] **HUD - HECM program statistics and limits** — hud.gov/stat/sfh/hecm
[3] **CFPB - Borrower responsibilities** — consumerfinance.gov/ask-cfpb/235
[4] **CFPB - Heirs and the home** — consumerfinance.gov/ask-cfpb/242
[5] **CFPB - Eligibility and property charges** — consumerfinance.gov/ask-cfpb/227
[6] **U.S. Code - Cross-selling safeguards** — uscode.house.gov - 12 USC 1715z-20
[7] **IRS - Excess-benefit transactions** — irs.gov/charities-non-profits
[8] **IRS - Rebuttable presumption** — irs.gov/charities-non-profits
[9] **NAIC - Life-insurance illustrations** — content.naic.org/insurance-topics

Sources last checked July 31, 2026. Verify current requirements, limits, links, and state-specific law before use.

Protect the Plan. Prepare the Family.

The strongest legacy strategy is documented, stress-tested, communicated, and reviewed every year.

PART II SUMMARY

Seven Principles to Carry Forward

1. **Start with the retirement objective—not the largest possible loan.**
2. **Replace every assumption with current written information.**
3. **Protect cash flow by planning for taxes, insurance, assessments, and maintenance.**
4. **Choose the draw structure that matches the documented need.**
5. **Keep mortgage, insurance, estate, tax, and governance advice independent.**
6. **Give heirs a realistic payoff, refinance, sale, and records plan.**
7. **Review the household, property, loan, insurance, and legacy plan every year.**

Next: use the workbook to replace generalized strategy with your household's verified facts, documents, questions, and decisions.

PART III

Retirement Finance & Expense Workbook

A large-print, handwriting-friendly planning workbook for household income, expenses, property costs, home equity, scenarios, documents, and decision preparation.

THE PULPIT & THE PEOPLE

Pathway Educational Resources

RETIREMENT FINANCE & EXPENSE WORKBOOK

ORGANIZE. PLAN. PREPARE. FOR A CONFIDENT RETIREMENT.

A large-print, handwriting-friendly planning workbook for household income, expenses, home equity, HECM education, and retirement decision preparation.

EDUCATIONAL RESOURCE

THIS WORKBOOK BELONGS TO

Keep this workbook with your important retirement-planning records.

Name	
Spouse / Partner	
Phone	
Email	
Home Address	
Date Started	
Date Last Updated	

What I hope to accomplish with this workbook

PLANNING NOTE

Review and update these pages whenever income, expenses, housing costs, insurance, health, family circumstances, or retirement goals change.

IMPORTANT EDUCATIONAL NOTICE

Read this page before using the worksheets.

This workbook is for educational and organizational purposes only. It is not a loan application, lender quote, financial plan, investment recommendation, legal opinion, tax advice, insurance recommendation, or guarantee of HECM eligibility or proceeds.

A Home Equity Conversion Mortgage (HECM) is a federally insured reverse-mortgage program with rules, costs, counseling requirements, borrower responsibilities, and eligibility standards that can change. Final figures must come from qualified professionals and current written documentation.

Property taxes, homeowners insurance, required assessments, and home maintenance remain ongoing homeowner obligations. A HECM generally does not eliminate these responsibilities.

Use this physical workbook to organize facts and questions before speaking with an FHA-approved HECM lender, an independent HUD-approved housing counselor, and appropriate legal, tax, insurance, and financial professionals.

CAUTION

Never rely on example rates, principal-limit factors, property values, projected appreciation, life expectancy, or insurance benefits when making a transaction decision. Replace estimates with verified information.

WORKBOOK NAVIGATION

Workbook Roadmap

Move through the workbook in order, then return to any section as needed.

PLANNING NOTE

The expanded educational sections now precede the workbook so readers can understand the HECM mechanics, risks, alternatives, spouse and heir issues, and case-study logic before entering their own household numbers.

Official source note: HUD HECM program materials; HUD housing-counseling guidance; and CFPB reverse-mortgage consumer guidance. Verify current rules and limits.

SECTION 1

HOUSEHOLD SNAPSHOT & GOALS

Start with the facts: who is in the household, what matters most, and what retirement must support.

Use a dark pen or pencil. Write clearly. Revisit these pages whenever your circumstances change.

SECTION 1

HOUSEHOLD SNAPSHOT

Record the people, ages, housing situation, and retirement stage that frame your decisions.

Homeowner / Borrower Age	
Spouse / Partner Age	
Other Household Members	
Current Retirement Status	Retired / Working / Part-time / Other
Years in Current Home	
Approximate Years You Hope to Remain	
Current Mortgage / Liens	
Emergency Savings	

Important family or household considerations

SECTION 1 RETIREMENT PRIORITIES

Rank the outcomes that matter most to you.

- ☐ Remain in my current home
- ☐ Reduce monthly financial pressure
- ☐ Build emergency reserves
- ☐ Pay off existing mortgage or liens
- ☐ Cover healthcare or caregiving costs
- ☐ Preserve flexibility for future needs
- ☐ Support a spouse or partner
- ☐ Leave the home or equity to heirs
- ☐ Fund home repairs or accessibility improvements
- ☐ Create a predictable retirement budget
- ☐ Reduce reliance on credit cards or personal loans
- ☐ Other: ______________________________

My top three priorities and why they matter

SECTION 2

INCOME & EXPENSES

Build a complete monthly picture before evaluating any retirement-finance strategy.

Use a dark pen or pencil. Write clearly. Revisit these pages whenever your circumstances change.

SECTION 2 MONTHLY INCOME — PAGE 1

Enter reliable monthly amounts before taxes unless otherwise noted.

Income Source	Homeowner / Spouse 1	Spouse 2	Other Household	Monthly Total	Notes
Social Security	$	$	$	$	
Pension / Retirement Plan	$	$	$	$	
Church Retirement Benefit	$	$	$	$	
Employment / Consulting	$	$	$	$	
Rental Income	$	$	$	$	
Investment / Dividend Income	$	$	$	$	

Income notes or timing considerations

SECTION 2 MONTHLY INCOME — PAGE 2

Include every recurring or reasonably expected income source.

Income Source	Homeowner / Spouse 1	Spouse 2	Other Household	Monthly Total	Notes
Annuity Income	$	$	$	$	
Business / Self-Employment	$	$	$	$	
Veterans / Disability Benefits	$	$	$	$	
Alimony / Support Received	$	$	$	$	
Required Minimum Distributions	$	$	$	$	
Other Income 1	$	$	$	$	
Other Income 2	$	$	$	$	

TOTAL MONTHLY HOUSEHOLD INCOME	$
ESTIMATED ANNUAL HOUSEHOLD INCOME	$

SECTION 2 MONTHLY EXPENSES — HOUSING & UTILITIES

Use current bills or a 3–6 month average.

Expense	Fixed / Variable	Essential?	Monthly Amount	Annual Amount	Notes
Property Taxes		☐ Yes ☐ No	$	$	
Homeowners / Hazard Insurance		☐ Yes ☐ No	$	$	
Flood Insurance (if applicable)		☐ Yes ☐ No	$	$	
HOA / Community Assessments		☐ Yes ☐ No	$	$	
Electricity / Gas		☐ Yes ☐ No	$	$	
Water / Sewer / Trash		☐ Yes ☐ No	$	$	
Telephone / Internet		☐ Yes ☐ No	$	$	
Home Maintenance Reserve		☐ Yes ☐ No	$	$	

SECTION 2 **MONTHLY EXPENSES — HOUSEHOLD & TRANSPORTATION**

Capture the routine expenses that support day-to-day living.

Expense	Fixed / Variable	Essential?	Monthly Amount	Annual Amount	Notes
Groceries		☐ Yes ☐ No	$	$	
Household Supplies		☐ Yes ☐ No	$	$	
Transportation / Fuel		☐ Yes ☐ No	$	$	
Vehicle Payment(s)		☐ Yes ☐ No	$	$	
Auto Insurance		☐ Yes ☐ No	$	$	
Parking / Tolls		☐ Yes ☐ No	$	$	
Pet Care		☐ Yes ☐ No	$	$	
Personal Care / Clothing		☐ Yes ☐ No	$	$	

SECTION 2 MONTHLY EXPENSES — HEALTH, DEBT & PROTECTION

Include premiums, debt payments, and recurring medical costs.

Expense	Fixed / Variable	Essential?	Monthly Amount	Annual Amount	Notes
Health Insurance / Medicare		☐ Yes ☐ No	$	$	
Medical Copays / Dental / Vision		☐ Yes ☐ No	$	$	
Prescriptions		☐ Yes ☐ No	$	$	
Credit Cards / Personal Loans		☐ Yes ☐ No	$	$	
Life Insurance Premiums		☐ Yes ☐ No	$	$	
Long-Term Care Premiums		☐ Yes ☐ No	$	$	
Legal / Financial / Professional		☐ Yes ☐ No	$	$	
Income / Estimated Taxes		☐ Yes ☐ No	$	$	

SECTION 2 **MONTHLY EXPENSES — LIFESTYLE & FAMILY**

Lifestyle spending matters because it determines the retirement you are actually trying to sustain.

Expense	Fixed / Variable	Essential?	Monthly Amount	Annual Amount	Notes
Church / Charitable Giving		☐ Yes ☐ No	$	$	
Dining / Entertainment		☐ Yes ☐ No	$	$	
Travel / Recreation		☐ Yes ☐ No	$	$	
Family Support / Gifts		☐ Yes ☐ No	$	$	
Hobbies / Memberships		☐ Yes ☐ No	$	$	
Emergency Savings Contribution		☐ Yes ☐ No	$	$	
Miscellaneous 1		☐ Yes ☐ No	$	$	
Miscellaneous 2		☐ Yes ☐ No	$	$	

SECTION 2 ANNUAL & IRREGULAR EXPENSES

Some of the largest retirement expenses are not monthly.

Irregular Expense	Expected Month	Estimated Amount	Savings Already Set Aside	Funding Plan
Property tax increase / special assessment		$	$	
Insurance deductible		$	$	
Major home repair		$	$	
HVAC / roof / appliances		$	$	
Vehicle repair or replacement		$	$	
Dental / hearing / vision		$	$	
Travel / family event		$	$	
Professional fees		$	$	
Holiday / gift spending		$	$	
Other		$	$	

SECTION 2 **HOUSEHOLD CASH-FLOW SUMMARY**

Bring the income and expense pages together.

Total Monthly Household Income	$
Total Monthly Household Expenses	$
Monthly Surplus / (Deficit)	$
Annual Surplus / (Deficit)	$
Essential Monthly Expenses	$
Discretionary Monthly Expenses	$
Monthly Property Charges	$

PLANNING NOTE

If expenses exceed income, first identify which expenses are essential, which are discretionary, and which are temporary. A HECM should not be treated as a substitute for understanding the underlying budget.

What stands out to me about our current cash flow

SECTION 2 EXPENSE REDUCTION WORKSHEET

Before borrowing, identify realistic opportunities to improve cash flow.

Expense to Review	Current Monthly Cost	Possible New Cost	Potential Monthly Savings	Action / Deadline
	$	$	$	
	$	$	$	
	$	$	$	
	$	$	$	
	$	$	$	
	$	$	$	
	$	$	$	
	$	$	$	
	$	$	$	
	$	$	$	

SECTION 3

HOME, PROPERTY COSTS & RESERVES

Protect the home by planning for the costs that continue before and after a HECM.

Use a dark pen or pencil. Write clearly. Revisit these pages whenever your circumstances change.

SECTION 3 **PROPERTY CHARGE PLANNER**

These obligations remain critical for homeowners.

Property Charge	Annual Amount	Due Date(s)	Paid From	Current?	Notes
Property Taxes	$			☐ Yes ☐ No	
Homeowners / Hazard Insurance	$			☐ Yes ☐ No	
Flood Insurance	$			☐ Yes ☐ No	
HOA / Condo Assessments	$			☐ Yes ☐ No	
Ground Rent / Leasehold Fees	$			☐ Yes ☐ No	
Other Required Property Charge	$			☐ Yes ☐ No	

PLANNING NOTE

Failure to keep required property charges current can create serious consequences. Verify exact responsibilities during HUD-approved counseling and with the lender.

SECTION 3
HOME MAINTENANCE & REPAIR RESERVE

Estimate what the home may reasonably require over the next several years.

Item	Condition	Estimated Timing	Estimated Cost	Savings Set Aside	Priority
Roof			$	$	
HVAC			$	$	
Plumbing			$	$	
Electrical			$	$	
Exterior / Paint			$	$	
Windows / Doors			$	$	
Appliances			$	$	
Accessibility / Safety			$	$	
Landscaping / Drainage			$	$	
Other			$	$	

SECTION 3

SECTION 3 EMERGENCY RESERVE PLANNER

Separate emergency cash from money earmarked for routine bills.

Current Emergency Cash	$
Target Emergency Reserve	$
Months of Essential Expenses Covered	
Monthly Amount We Can Add	$
Where Reserve Is Held	
Who Can Access It in an Emergency	

Emergencies we specifically want to be prepared for

SECTION 3 # HOME & MORTGAGE SNAPSHOT

Use current statements and property records.

Property Address	
Estimated / Appraised Value	$
Current Mortgage Balance	$
Second Mortgage / HELOC Balance	$
Other Liens	$
Current Interest Rate	%
Monthly Principal & Interest	$
Approximate Home Equity	$
Title / Ownership Names	
Homestead / Primary Residence Status	

SECTION 3
HOME EQUITY GOALS

Define what you want the home to accomplish for you.

- ☐ Remain in home for life if practical
- ☐ Create monthly cash-flow flexibility
- ☐ Pay off current mortgage payment
- ☐ Fund repairs or accessibility upgrades
- ☐ Build a reserve for healthcare or emergencies
- ☐ Create a line of credit for future needs
- ☐ Preserve as much equity as practical
- ☐ Leave home to heirs
- ☐ Sell or downsize later
- ☐ Undecided / need professional guidance

My thoughts about using home equity in retirement

SECTION 4

HECM PLANNING WORKSHEETS

Organize verified facts, questions, and possible uses before making any decision.

Use a dark pen or pencil. Write clearly. Revisit these pages whenever your circumstances change.

SECTION 4 HECM INFORMATION & ASSUMPTIONS

Use verified lender/counselor information whenever available.

Homeowner / Borrower Age	years
Spouse / Partner Age	years
Appraised / Qualifying Property Value	$
Current Program Maximum Claim Amount	$
Existing Liens / Mortgage Payoff	$
Estimated Closing Costs	$
Expected Interest + Ongoing MIP Rate	%
Estimated Gross Principal Limit	$
Estimated Net HECM Funds	$
Emergency Cash Outside HECM	$

PLANNING NOTE

Do not estimate the principal limit factor yourself for a transaction. The lender determines the actual principal limit using current program rules, age, expected rate, property value, and other requirements.

SECTION 4 **HECM COST & OBLIGATION WORKSHEET**

List each cost or continuing obligation you want explained.

Item	Quoted / Estimated Amount	Financed?	Who Verified It?	Questions / Notes
Origination Charge	$	☐ Yes ☐ No		
Initial Mortgage Insurance Premium	$	☐ Yes ☐ No		
Appraisal	$	☐ Yes ☐ No		
Title / Settlement	$	☐ Yes ☐ No		
Recording / Government Fees	$	☐ Yes ☐ No		
Counseling Fee (if any)	$	☐ Yes ☐ No		
Servicing / Other Fees	$	☐ Yes ☐ No		
Existing Liens to Pay Off	$	☐ Yes ☐ No		
Repairs / Set-Asides	$	☐ Yes ☐ No		
Other	$	☐ Yes ☐ No		

SECTION 4 POSSIBLE USE OF FUNDS

Prioritize needs before discussing payout options.

Possible Use	Priority 1–5	Estimated Amount	One-Time or Ongoing?	Notes
Pay off existing mortgage / lien		$		
Emergency reserve		$		
Home repairs / accessibility		$		
Healthcare / caregiving		$		
Monthly budget supplement		$		
Debt reduction		$		
Property-charge reserve		$		
Future line-of-credit needs		$		
Family / legacy purpose		$		
Other		$		

SECTION 4 **PAYOUT OPTION QUESTIONS**

Use this page to compare options after counseling and lender explanation.

Option	How It Works	Advantages for Us	Tradeoffs / Risks	Questions
Line of credit				
Monthly tenure payment				
Monthly term payment				
Lump sum / initial draw				
Combination of options				

SECTION 4

CURRENT MORTGAGE PAYOFF PLANNING

Understand what changes if an existing mortgage is paid at HECM closing.

Current Monthly Mortgage Payment	$
Verified Payoff Amount	$
Estimated HECM Funds Used for Payoff	$
Monthly Cash Flow Freed	$
Other Debts Paid at Closing	$
Estimated Funds Remaining After Payoff / Costs	$

Questions or concerns about paying off the existing mortgage

SECTION 4 **BORROWER RESPONSIBILITIES CHECKLIST**

Confirm these responsibilities in counseling and lender documents.

☐ Occupy the home as the required principal residence

☐ Pay property taxes on time

☐ Maintain required homeowners / hazard insurance

☐ Pay required HOA / condominium assessments

☐ Maintain the home in acceptable condition

☐ Comply with loan-document requirements

☐ Respond to annual occupancy or certification requests

☐ Understand what may cause the loan to become due and payable

☐ Keep important loan and counseling documents

☐ Tell trusted family / heirs where records are kept

Responsibilities I need explained further

SECTION 5

SCENARIOS & LONG-TERM PLANNING

Compare alternatives instead of relying on one set of assumptions.

Use a dark pen or pencil. Write clearly. Revisit these pages whenever your circumstances change.

SECTION 5 **SCENARIO A — CURRENT PLAN**

Use verified figures where possible; otherwise clearly label estimates.

Monthly Household Income	$
Monthly Household Expenses	$
Monthly Surplus / (Deficit)	$
Initial HECM Draw / Payoff	$
Ongoing Monthly HECM Draw	$
Emergency Cash Remaining	$
Estimated Home Value	$
Estimated HECM Balance at Milestone	$

What this scenario would mean for our lifestyle, home, and family

SECTION 5 **SCENARIO B — LOWER-INCOME / HIGHER-EXPENSE CASE**

Use verified figures where possible; otherwise clearly label estimates.

Monthly Household Income	$
Monthly Household Expenses	$
Monthly Surplus / (Deficit)	$
Initial HECM Draw / Payoff	$
Ongoing Monthly HECM Draw	$
Emergency Cash Remaining	$
Estimated Home Value	$
Estimated HECM Balance at Milestone	$

What this scenario would mean for our lifestyle, home, and family

SECTION 5 # SCENARIO C — ALTERNATIVE STRATEGY

Use verified figures where possible; otherwise clearly label estimates.

Monthly Household Income	$
Monthly Household Expenses	$
Monthly Surplus / (Deficit)	$
Initial HECM Draw / Payoff	$
Ongoing Monthly HECM Draw	$
Emergency Cash Remaining	$
Estimated Home Value	$
Estimated HECM Balance at Milestone	$

What this scenario would mean for our lifestyle, home, and family

SECTION 5 SCENARIO COMPARISON

Place your three scenarios side-by-side.

Metric	Scenario A	Scenario B	Scenario C	Best Fit / Why
Monthly Surplus / Deficit				
Existing Mortgage Payment Eliminated?				
Emergency Reserve				
Projected HECM Reliance				
Home Equity Preservation				
Flexibility for Future Needs				
Comfort Level				
Professional Concerns				

SECTION 5
INCOME CHANGE STRESS TEST

Explore what happens if household income changes.

Income Change	Adjusted Monthly Income	Monthly Expenses	Monthly Surplus / Deficit	Possible HECM Draw Need	Notes
-30%	$	$	$	$	
-20%	$	$	$	$	
-10%	$	$	$	$	
Current	$	$	$	$	
+10%	$	$	$	$	
+20%	$	$	$	$	
+30%	$	$	$	$	

PLANNING NOTE

Income changes do not directly determine the HECM principal limit. This exercise is about how changing income can affect household cash flow and the amount a household might need to draw over time.

SECTION 5
EXPENSE INFLATION STRESS TEST

Test whether the plan still works if living costs rise faster than expected.

Expense Increase	Adjusted Monthly Expenses	Monthly Income	Monthly Surplus / Deficit	What Would We Change?
Current	$	$	$	
+5%	$	$	$	
+10%	$	$	$	
+15%	$	$	$	
+20%	$	$	$	
+25%	$	$	$	

SECTION 5 **HOME VALUE MILESTONE PLANNER**

Use conservative assumptions; appreciation is never guaranteed.

Milestone	Estimated Home Value	Assumption Used	Source / Reason	Notes
Today	$			
Year 5	$			
Year 10	$			
Year 15	$			
Year 20	$			
Year 25	$			
Year 30	$			

SECTION 5 HECM BALANCE MILESTONE PLANNER

Record lender illustrations or your own clearly labeled educational estimates.

Milestone	Beginning Balance	Draws Added	Interest / MIP Added	Ending Balance	Verified / Estimated?
Today	$	$	$	$	
Year 5	$	$	$	$	
Year 10	$	$	$	$	
Year 15	$	$	$	$	
Year 20	$	$	$	$	
Year 25	$	$	$	$	
Year 30	$	$	$	$	

SECTION 5 30-YEAR PLANNING MILESTONES

Focus on decision points rather than pretending any 30-year forecast is guaranteed.

Year	Income Outlook	Expense Outlook	Home / Repair Need	HECM / Cash Need	Family / Legacy Note
1					
5					
10					
15					
20					
25					
30					

SECTION 5 **INSURANCE & LEGACY PLANNING**

If insurance is part of the strategy, use carrier-issued information only.

Life Insurance Carrier	
Policy Type	
Current Death Benefit	$
Current Premium	$
Policy Owner	
Beneficiary / Beneficiaries	
Illustration Date	
Professional Who Reviewed Policy	

How insurance is intended to fit into our retirement / legacy plan

PLANNING NOTE

Life-insurance performance, premiums, policy values, and death benefits depend on the specific contract and carrier. Do not treat an illustration as a guarantee.

SECTION 6

FAMILY, PROFESSIONALS & DOCUMENTS

Good retirement decisions are easier when important people and records are organized.

Use a dark pen or pencil. Write clearly. Revisit these pages whenever your circumstances change.

SECTION 6 **FAMILY & HEIRS CONVERSATION**

Write down what you want your family to understand.

- ☐ We have discussed whether we want to remain in the home
- ☐ Heirs understand a HECM loan balance may grow over time
- ☐ Family knows where mortgage / HECM documents are stored
- ☐ We have discussed what happens if the home is sold
- ☐ We have discussed what happens after the last borrower leaves the home permanently
- ☐ Heirs know which professionals to contact
- ☐ We have discussed estate / title issues with an attorney if appropriate
- ☐ We have documented our wishes rather than relying only on verbal conversations

Topics we still need to discuss

SECTION 6 DOCUMENTS TO GATHER

Bring copies—not originals unless specifically requested.

- ☐ Government-issued identification
- ☐ Social Security / retirement income statements
- ☐ Pension / annuity statements
- ☐ Recent bank / investment statements
- ☐ Mortgage statement and payoff information
- ☐ Property tax bill
- ☐ Homeowners / flood insurance declarations
- ☐ HOA / condominium statement
- ☐ Property deed / title information
- ☐ Recent appraisal or property-value evidence
- ☐ Debt statements
- ☐ Life-insurance policy / current illustration
- ☐ Estate-planning documents
- ☐ Power of attorney / healthcare documents
- ☐ Other

Documents I still need to locate

SECTION 6 **QUESTIONS FOR A HUD-APPROVED HECM COUNSELOR**

QUESTIONS FOR A HUD-APPROVED HECM COUNSELOR

Take this page to counseling.

- ☐ What are the major HECM options and alternatives for our situation?
- ☐ What borrower responsibilities continue after closing?
- ☐ What events can cause the loan to become due and payable?
- ☐ How could a non-borrowing spouse be affected?
- ☐ How do taxes, insurance, assessments, and maintenance affect the loan?
- ☐ What should our heirs understand?
- ☐ What alternatives should we compare before deciding?
- ☐ What questions should we ask the lender before signing anything?

Counselor answers / notes

SECTION 6 QUESTIONS FOR THE HECM LENDER

Ask for written explanations and itemized figures.

- ☐ What property value is being used and why?
- ☐ What expected rate and principal limit apply?
- ☐ What are all upfront and ongoing costs?
- ☐ Which costs are financed into the loan?
- ☐ How much must be used to pay existing liens?
- ☐ What payout options are available?
- ☐ How does the line of credit work under the proposed loan?
- ☐ What servicing requirements should we expect?
- ☐ What assumptions are used in the lender illustration?
- ☐ What documents should we keep after closing?

Lender answers / notes

SECTION 6 **QUESTIONS FOR LEGAL, TAX, INSURANCE & FINANCIAL PROFESSIONALS**

HECM decisions can affect more than the mortgage itself.

Professional	Question / Issue	Answer / Recommendation	Follow-Up
Attorney			
CPA / Tax Professional			
Insurance Professional			
Financial Professional			
Estate Planner			
Other			

SECTION 6 PROFESSIONAL CONTACT LOG

Keep names, licenses, organizations, and contact information together.

Role	Name / Organization	Phone	Email	Date Contacted
HUD Counselor				
HECM Lender				
Attorney				
CPA / Tax Professional				
Insurance Professional				
Financial Professional				
Other				

SECTION 7

DECISION READINESS & ACTION PLAN

Use the final pages to decide what is verified, what is unresolved, and what happens next.

Use a dark pen or pencil. Write clearly. Revisit these pages whenever your circumstances change.

SECTION 7 DECISION READINESS CHECKLIST

Do not rush past unanswered questions.

☐ Household income is verified
☐ Household expenses are complete and realistic
☐ Property taxes and insurance are current
☐ Home repair needs have been reviewed
☐ Emergency reserves are understood
☐ Mortgage / lien payoff amounts are verified
☐ HUD-approved counseling is completed or scheduled
☐ Lender figures are in writing
☐ All major costs have been explained
☐ Spouse / partner implications are understood
☐ Heirs / family concerns have been discussed
☐ Legal / tax / insurance questions are addressed where appropriate
☐ We compared alternatives to a HECM
☐ We understand borrower responsibilities
☐ We feel no pressure to make an immediate decision

SECTION 7 MY DECISION SUMMARY

Summarize what you understand before committing to any course of action.

Strategy I Am Considering	
Why It May Help	
Biggest Benefit	
Biggest Tradeoff	
Most Important Unanswered Question	
Professional I Need to Speak With Next	
Decision Deadline (if any)	

My own words: why this strategy does or does not fit our household

SECTION 7 **30-DAY ACTION PLAN**

Turn planning into specific next steps.

Priority	Action	Who Is Responsible?	Target Date	Status
1				☐ Not Started ☐ Done
2				☐ Not Started ☐ Done
3				☐ Not Started ☐ Done
4				☐ Not Started ☐ Done
5				☐ Not Started ☐ Done
6				☐ Not Started ☐ Done
7				☐ Not Started ☐ Done
8				☐ Not Started ☐ Done
9				☐ Not Started ☐ Done
10				☐ Not Started ☐ Done

SECTION 7 NOTES — PAGE 1

Use for counseling, lender calls, family meetings, or personal reflections.

SECTION 7 NOTES — PAGE 2

Date each note so you can follow your decision process over time.

SECTION 7 **FINAL PLANNING SUMMARY**

Keep this page at the front of your records after you complete the workbook.

Total Monthly Income	$
Total Monthly Expenses	$
Monthly Surplus / Deficit	$
Emergency Reserve	$
Current Mortgage / Liens	$
Estimated Property Value	$
HECM Strategy Being Considered	
Next Professional Appointment	
Next Action Date	

My final notes before the next decision point

IMPORTANT
Educational resource only. Final HECM eligibility, proceeds, rates, fees, servicing terms, and borrower obligations are determined by current program rules and the lender's verified transaction documents. Independent HUD-approved counseling is an important part of the HECM process.

OFFICIAL REFERENCE RESOURCES

Use current official sources when program rules or responsibilities need to be verified.

Topic	Official Source
HUD — Home Equity Conversion Mortgages	https://www.hud.gov/hud-partners/single-family-hecmhome
Consumer Financial Protection Bureau — Reverse Mortgages	https://www.consumerfinance.gov/consumer-tools/reverse-mortgages/
CFPB — Borrower Responsibilities	https://www.consumerfinance.gov/ask-cfpb/what-are-my-responsibilities-as-a-reverse-mortgage-loan-borrower-en-235/
CFPB — Heirs and the Home	https://www.consumerfinance.gov/ask-cfpb/with-a-reverse-mortgage-loan-can-my-heirs-keep-or-sell-my-home-after-i-die-en-242/

PATHWAY EDUCATIONAL RESOURCES

Organize the facts. Ask better questions. Make informed retirement decisions.

QUICK REFERENCE

Plain-Language Glossary

FHA	The Federal Housing Administration, which insures HECMs that meet program requirements.
HECM	Home Equity Conversion Mortgage — the FHA-insured reverse-mortgage program.
HUD-APPROVED COUNSELOR	An independent housing counselor approved by HUD to provide required HECM counseling.
PRINCIPAL LIMIT	The maximum initial amount available before deductions, based on program factors such as age, expected rate, and qualifying property value.
NET PROCEEDS	Funds remaining after required payoffs, financed costs, set-asides, and other deductions.
LINE OF CREDIT	An available borrowing structure that permits eligible future draws, subject to the loan terms.
NON-RECOURSE	Generally, neither the borrower nor the estate owes more than the home's value when the loan becomes due and payable, subject to program rules.
FINANCIAL ASSESSMENT	The lender's review of the borrower's capacity and willingness to meet property-charge and loan obligations.
LESA	Life Expectancy Set-Aside — funds reserved from proceeds to help pay certain property charges when required.
DUE AND PAYABLE	The point at which the loan must be resolved, commonly after the last borrower permanently leaves the home, dies, sells, or fails to meet loan obligations.
MIP	Mortgage insurance premium paid in connection with FHA insurance.
RIGHT OF RESCISSION	For many HECM refinances, a three-business-day period after closing during which the borrower may cancel; purchase transactions differ.

COORDINATION CHECKLIST

Build the Right Professional Team

No single professional should be expected to answer every mortgage, tax, legal, insurance, estate, and household-planning question.

- ☐ **HUD-approved housing counselor**

  Independent education, alternatives, costs, obligations, and counseling certificate.

- ☐ **FHA-approved HECM lender**

  Current eligibility review, written estimates, financial assessment, appraisal, costs, and loan terms.

- ☐ **Estate-planning attorney**

  Title, spouse and heir protections, trusts, powers of attorney, probate, and payoff planning.

- ☐ **Tax professional**

  Tax treatment, property transfer, compensation, benefits, deductions, and reporting questions.

- ☐ **Insurance professional**

  Separate underwriting, guarantees, premium duration, beneficiaries, lapse risk, and carrier strength.

- ☐ **Financial professional**

  Cash flow, reserves, investments, longevity, retirement income, alternatives, and scenario testing.

- ☐ **Family decision participant**

MEETING STANDARD

Ask for written figures, note the date and source of each answer, disclose relevant conflicts, and do not sign until the documents match what you understand.

CONTINUE WITH CURRENT INFORMATION

Official Resources & Companion Toolkit

Use primary sources for current program guidance, then scan the QR code to reach the complete Pathway educational toolkit and companion resources.

HUD HECM information	hud.gov/hud-partners/single-family-reverse-mortgages
HUD counselor search	hud.gov/housing-counseling
Consumer Financial Protection Bureau	consumerfinance.gov/consumer-tools/reverse-mortgages
FHA lender search	hud.gov/lender-list
AnnualCreditReport	annualcreditreport.com

Continue Your Pathway

Scan to visit The Pulpit & The People Home Resource and Knowledge page for current HECM education, official-resource links, articles, and companion planning information.

ISBN 979-8-9967481-2-9

Verify that the destination is correct before entering personal information.

www.ingramcontent.com/pod-product-compliance
Lightning Source LLC
LaVergne TN
LVHW070625061126
851857LV00002B/12
* 9 7 9 8 9 9 6 7 4 8 1 2 9 *